An Analysis of

Oliver Sacks's

The Man Who Mistook His Wife for a Hat and Other Clinical Tales

Dario Krpan
with
Alexander J. O'Connor

ROUTLEDGE

Copyright © 2017 by Macat International Ltd
24:13 Coda Centre, 189 Munster Road, London SW6 6AW.

Macat International has asserted its right under the Copyright, Designs and Patents Act
1988 to be identified as the copyright holder of this work.

www.macat.com
info@macat.com

Cover illustration: Martin Ross

Cataloguing in Publication Data
A catalogue record for this book is available from the British Library.
Library of Congress Cataloguing-in-Publication Data is available upon request.

ISBN 978-1-912303-66-3 (hardback)
ISBN 978-1-912128-46-4 (paperback)
ISBN 978-1-912282-54-8 (e-book)

Notice
The information in this book is designed to orientate readers of the work under analysis,
to elucidate and contextualise its key ideas and themes, and to aid in the development
of critical thinking skills. It is not meant to be used, nor should it be used, as a
substitute for original thinking or in place of original writing or research. References and
notes are provided for informational purposes and their presence does not constitute
endorsement of the information or opinions therein. This book is presented solely for
educational purposes. It is sold on the understanding that the publisher is not engaged
to provide any scholarly advice. The publisher has made every effort to ensure that
this book is accurate and up-to-date, but makes no warranties or representations with
regard to the completeness or reliability of the information it contains. The information
and the opinions provided herein are not guaranteed or warranted to produce particular
results and may not be suitable for students of every ability. The publisher shall not be
liable for any loss, damage or disruption arising from any errors or omissions, or from
the use of this book, including, but not limited to, special, incidental, consequential or
other damages caused, or alleged to have been caused, directly or indirectly, by the
information contained within.

CONTENTS

THE MACAT LIBRARY

The Macat Library is a series of unique academic explorations of seminal works in the humanities and social sciences – books and papers that have had a significant and widely recognised impact on their disciplines. It has been created to serve as much more than just a summary of what lies between the covers of a great book. It illuminates and explores the influences on, ideas of, and impact of that book. Our goal is to offer a learning resource that encourages critical thinking and fosters a better, deeper understanding of important ideas.

Each publication is divided into three Sections: Influences, Ideas, and Impact. Each Section has four Modules. These explore every important facet of the work, and the responses to it.

This Section-Module structure makes a Macat Library book easy to use, but it has another important feature. Because each Macat book is written to the same format, it is possible (and encouraged!) to cross-reference multiple Macat books along the same lines of inquiry or research. This allows the reader to open up interesting interdisciplinary pathways.

To further aid your reading, lists of glossary terms and people mentioned are included at the end of this book (these are indicated by an asterisk [*] throughout) – as well as a list of works cited.

Macat has worked with the University of Cambridge to identify the elements of critical thinking and understand the ways in which six different skills combine to enable effective thinking.
Three allow us to fully understand a problem; three more give us the tools to solve it. Together, these six skills make up the **PACIER** model of critical thinking. They are:

ANALYSIS – understanding how an argument is built
EVALUATION – exploring the strengths and weaknesses of an argument
INTERPRETATION – understanding issues of meaning

CREATIVE THINKING – coming up with new ideas and fresh connections
PROBLEM-SOLVING – producing strong solutions
REASONING – creating strong arguments

To find out more, visit **WWW.MACAT.COM.**

CRITICAL THINKING AND *THE MAN WHO MISTOOK HIS WIFE FOR A HAT*

Primary critical thinking skill: CREATIVE THINKING
Secondary critical thinking skill: REASONING

In *The Man Who Mistook His Wife for a Hat*, neurologist Oliver Sacks looked at the cutting-edge work taking place in his field, and decided that much of it was not fit for purpose. Sacks found it hard to understand why most doctors adopted a mechanical and impersonal approach to their patients, and opened his mind to new ways to treat people with neurological disorders. He explored the question of deciding what such new ways might be by deploying his formidable creative thinking skills. Sacks felt the issues at the heart of patient care needed redefining, because the way they were being dealt with hurt not only patients, but practitioners too. They limited a physician's capacity to understand and then treat a patient's condition. To highlight the issue, Sacks wrote the stories of 24 patients and their neurological clinical conditions. In the process, he rebelled against traditional methodology by focusing on his patients' subjective experiences. Sacks did not only write about his patients in original ways – he attempt to come up with creative ways of treating them as well. At root, his method was to try to help each person individually, with the core aim of finding meaning and a sense of identity despite, or even thanks to, the patients' condition. Sacks thus redefined the issue of neurological work in a new way, and his ideas were so influential that they heralded the arrival of a broader movement – narrative medicine – that placed stronger emphasis on listening to and incorporating patients' experiences and insights into their care.

ABOUT THE AUTHOR OF THE ORIGINAL WORK

Oliver Sacks was born in Cricklewood, London in 1933. He left the United Kingdom at age 27 after receiving his medical degree from Oxford, and moved to California. There he engaged in what he called 'staggering bouts of pharmacological experimentation,' chiefly with hallucinogenic drugs, and this would influence his later writing about neurological states. Sacks relocated to New York City in the mid-1960s and began a long association with New York University. His second book, *Awakenings* (1973), detailed his experiences with patients suffering from a neurological condition caused by a virus that led to long-lasting coma. A successful movie of the book was released in 1990. Sacks published 11 books, and *The Man Who Mistook His Wife for a Hat* (1985) was his first *New York Times* best seller. Sacks was a renowned public intellectual and a frequent contributor to the *New Yorker* and the *London Review of Books*. He died in August 2015 at the age of 82.

ABOUT THE AUTHORS OF THE ANALYSIS

Dr Dario Krpan holds a PhD in psychology from the University of Cambridge. He is currently a Fellow in behavioural science at the London School of Economics.

Dr Alexander O'Connor did his postgraduate work at the University of California, Berkeley, where he received a PhD for work on social and personality psychology.

ABOUT MACAT

GREAT WORKS FOR CRITICAL THINKING

Macat is focused on making the ideas of the world's great thinkers accessible and comprehensible to everybody, everywhere, in ways that promote the development of enhanced critical thinking skills.

It works with leading academics from the world's top universities to produce new analyses that focus on the ideas and the impact of the most influential works ever written across a wide variety of academic disciplines. Each of the works that sit at the heart of its growing library is an enduring example of great thinking. But by setting them in context – and looking at the influences that shaped their authors, as well as the responses they provoked – Macat encourages readers to look at these classics and game-changers with fresh eyes. Readers learn to think, engage and challenge their ideas, rather than simply accepting them.

'Macat offers an amazing first-of-its-kind tool for interdisciplinary learning and research. Its focus on works that transformed their disciplines and its rigorous approach, drawing on the world's leading experts and educational institutions, opens up a world-class education to anyone.'

Andreas Schleicher
Director for Education and Skills, Organisation for Economic Co-operation and Development

'Macat is taking on some of the major challenges in university education … They have drawn together a strong team of active academics who are producing teaching materials that are novel in the breadth of their approach.'

Prof Lord Broers,
former Vice-Chancellor of the University of Cambridge

'The Macat vision is exceptionally exciting. It focuses upon new modes of learning which analyse and explain seminal texts which have profoundly influenced world thinking and so social and economic development. It promotes the kind of critical thinking which is essential for any society and economy.
This is the learning of the future.'

Rt Hon Charles Clarke, former UK Secretary of State for Education

'The Macat analyses provide immediate access to the critical conversation surrounding the books that have shaped their respective discipline, which will make them an invaluable resource to all of those, students and teachers, working in the field.'

Professor William Tronzo, University of California at San Diego

WAYS IN TO THE TEXT

KEY POINTS

- Oliver Sacks was an English neurologist*—an expert in diseases and disorders of the nervous system—who was born in 1933. He spent most of his medical and professional career in the United States.

- *The Man Who Mistook His Wife for a Hat* argues for neurologists to revisit the use of narrative case studies*—detailed descriptions of a particular disorder, in the form of life stories—and for the value of considering patients' subjective experiences and insights.

- In supplying the reader with such insights, *The Man Who Mistook His Wife for a Hat* provides a unique opportunity to appreciate people who are often misunderstood.

Who Was Oliver Sacks?

Oliver Sacks, the author of *The Man Who Mistook His Wife for a Hat* (1985), was born in 1933 in England. His parents and brothers were medical doctors. Sacks obtained his medical degree from the University of Oxford in England before he moved to the United States, where he completed his postgraduate training and worked as a neurologist in various hospitals. At his death in August 2015, he was a professor of neurology at New York University.

Interviewed in 1997, Sacks recalled that his reasons for moving to the United States partly stemmed from differences in the medical culture: "I thought of medicine as less tightly organized here [the US]. In England, there seemed to be a rather strict hierarchy in academic medicine."[1]

Sacks was interested in abstract and subjective experiences—that is, experiences that belong to the experiencer alone—and spent much of his 20s and 30s abusing drugs in an attempt to expand his mind and consciousness.* In his 2015 memoir *On the Move: A Life*, he noted of his early drug abuse: "Such experiences, I thought, might help me understand what some of my patients were going through."[2] This desire to comprehend, and later to express, the experiences of his patients would define his life's mission, and form the theme of many of his later texts.

For Sacks, this focus was influenced and supported by his mentor and friend, the neuropsychologist Alexander R. Luria,* who advocated a similar patient-centered* approach to medicine (an approach to patient care that emphasized the importance of the individual patient's condition and needs). Sacks's books in this vein would become best-selling works of popular science,* and fame followed. A historian of medicine wrote in her analysis of Sacks's scientific contribution that "Oliver Sacks is actually one of the world's most famous neurologists,"[3] a mantle no one would dispute before his death on August 30, 2015.

What Does *The Man Who Mistook His Wife for a Hat* Say?

Sacks was concerned that neurology had developed a mechanical and impersonal approach to patient care unlike that of the past: "The tradition of richly human clinical tales," he writes, "reached a high point in the nineteenth century, and then declined, with the advent of an impersonal neurological science."[4] In fact, Sacks worried that such an impersonal approach limited a physician's ability to understand and treat a patient's condition. And so with *The Man Who Mistook His Wife*, as he had with his earlier 1973 text *Awakenings*, Sacks adopts the narrative case study. He writes the stories of 24 patients and their neurological clinical conditions—but focusing on the patients' subjective experience.

Sacks aims to detail how each patient struggled with his or her condition, both physically and psychologically. He discusses a patient with the pseudonym Jimmie G., for example, who suffered from extreme memory loss that froze him in the year 1945. Sacks and other physicians failed to improve Jimmie G.'s memory. So, with encouragement from Luria, Sacks decided to help him in other ways; he encouraged Jimmie G. and watched him re-engage with activities in which he found pleasure—playing games, going to church, gardening. Sacks described Jimmie G.'s improvement over the course of nine years of treatment and consultation: "Humanly, spiritually, he is at times a different man altogether—no longer fluttering, restless, bored, and lost, but deeply attentive to the beauty and soul of the world."[5] This all unfolded despite Jimmie G.'s memory not improving.

Though the patients, conditions, experiences, and Sacks's treatments differ in all two dozen case studies, Sacks attempts to highlight the condition from each patient's experience. Further, Sacks tries to explore how each one finds meaning and a sense of identity despite, or even thanks to, his or her condition.

The work became relevant in two principal ways. First, it introduced the public to neurological conditions, and the experiences associated with them, that had previously had very little exposure indeed. And second, the work heralded a broader movement—narrative medicine*—that placed stronger emphasis on listening to and incorporating patients' experiences and insights in their care.

As evidence of its influence in the medical community, *The Man Who Mistook His Wife*, alongside several of Sacks's other works, are recommended as part of the curricula for training physicians. Further, those advancing narrative medicine regard it as a seminal work crucial to improving the physician-patient relationship. One reviewer of Sacks's works, and *The Man Who Mistook His Wife for a Hat* in particular, wrote that as a neurologist "he has created a distinctive ethos and a personal medical ethic;"[6] more, as a writer, "Sacks is often credited with transforming a clinical genre, the case history, into a literary one and, in the process depathologizing his subjects"[7]—that is, his patients were no longer defined by their symptoms and their status as individuals was returned to them.

Sacks's text has been cited more than 2,500 times. More impressive has been its acceptance by the public; the work made the *New York Times* best-seller list on its initial release in 1985. *The Man Who Mistook His Wife* was the first encounter many readers had with several neurological conditions, as the conditions detailed by Sacks often rank among the most rare.

Why Does *The Man Who Mistook His Wife for a Hat* Matter?

The Man Who Mistook His Wife provides readers with a brief introduction to a range of topics; primarily, it outlines several rare neurological conditions.

Sacks details several types of memory loss along with conditions such as agnosia* (an inability to recognize specific objects, such as faces) and Tourette's syndrome* (which involves motor impulse excesses that result in tics, grimaces, and uncontrollable vocalizations). He also includes some medical descriptions to convey what occurs in the brains and bodies of the patients. But he then goes deeper, recreating the subjective experiences inside the patients' minds, as well as with their personalities and social lives.

Sacks hoped that the book would serve as a cross between science and literature: "The scientific and the romantic in such realms cry out to come together—Luria liked to speak here of 'romantic science.'They come together at the intersection of fact and fable, the intersection which characterizes ... the lives of the patients here narrated."[8]

Sacks saw those in his care as, first of all, people who found unique methods to cope with their conditions and struggled to find meaning. When this is related to the public, he believes, it can profoundly alter the general view of what it means to have a neurological disorder. In a 2012 interview he explained: "I think it's important that nature can put a positive spin on so many awful-seeming situations."[9] As an example, he included in the work a few cases of patients experiencing hallucinations,* and was cautious not to portray these as wholly negative. He also provided some insight into this approach: "People are scared of hallucinations—the very word immediately makes people aware of dementia or insanity. One of my more conscious motives is to provide some reassurance."[10]

Sacks's vision of a new neurology and science is somewhat realized today in the medium of popular science, and *The Man Who Mistook His Wife* represents one of its earliest and more successful examples. The book also provides readers with a unique opportunity to understand people with neurological conditions better, changing the thinking of readers in the process.

NOTES

1 Sandee Brawarsky, "Street Neurologist with a Sense of Wonder," *The Lancet* 350, no. 9084 (1997): 1092.

2 Oliver Sacks, *On the Move: A Life* (New York: Alfred A. Knopf, 2015), 115.

3 Daniela Mergenthaler, "Oliver Sacks—A Neurologist Explores the Lifeworld," *Medicine, Health Care and Philosophy* 3, no. 3 (2000): 275.

4 Oliver Sacks, *The Man Who Mistook His Wife for a Hat and Other Clinical Tales* (New York: Touchstone, 1998), viii.

5 Sacks, *The Man Who Mistook His Wife*, 32.

6   G. Thomas Couser, *Vulnerable Subjects: Ethics and Life Writing* (New York: Cornell University Press, 2004), 75.

7   Couser, *Vulnerable Subjects*, 75.

8   Sacks, *The Man Who Mistook His Wife*, ix.

9   David Wallace-Wells, "A Brain With a Heart," *New York Magazine*, November 4, 2012, accessed September 22, 2015, http://nymag.com/news/features/oliver-sacks-2012-11/.

10 Wallace-Wells, "A Brain With a Heart."

SECTION 1
INFLUENCES

MODULE 1
THE AUTHOR AND THE
HISTORICAL CONTEXT

KEY POINTS

- *The Man Who Mistook His Wife for a Hat* (1985) by Oliver Sacks heralded a patient-centered* movement in medicine—an approach to treatment that emphasizes the patient's specific needs and experience.

- Intrigued by considerations of subjective experiences (that is, experiences that belong uniquely to the individual), at one period Sacks experimented with certain drugs.

- Sacks moved to California in the 1960s, a time and place known for its permissive social and cultural lifestyles.

Why Read This Text?

The Man Who Mistook His Wife for a Hat by Oliver Sacks collects 24 short studies that explore the subjective experiences of his patients who suffered from neurological conditions*—conditions of the functioning of the brain and the nervous system that typically alter the thinking, memory, and sensations of those they afflict. Sacks was dismayed that these people were frequently perceived through the prism of their disorders—even by their neurologists* and physicians.* This motivated him to portray them as complete human beings, in the process devoting much of the text to exploring their identities, experiences, and struggles to cope with their conditions.

The text became a best seller and introduced several rare neurological disorders, such as Tourette's syndrome*—a condition characterized by things such as physical tics and uncontrollable vocalizations—to the general public. And although it was his fourth

> ❝ It was crucial for me to find something with
> meaning, and this, for me, was seeing patients. ❞
>
> Oliver Sacks, *On the Move: A Life*

book, *The Man Who Mistook His Wife* cemented Sacks's status as one of the world's most famous neurologists.

Further, the text "would mark the beginning of another career, and a much more public one, as perhaps the unlikeliest ambassador for brain science,"[1] according to one of Sacks's many profilers. In this way, the text established Sacks as a literary figure who communicated brain science to the public. And by focusing on how such disorders impact people's identity and day-to-day life, Sacks challenged the prevailing approach to patient care in neurology—which helped pave the way for a movement that today considers a patient's personal narratives in medical treatment.

Author's Life

Sacks was born in 1933 in London, England; his last professional position was as a professor of neurology at New York University. He noted in his memoir *On the Move: A Life* (2015) that his career in medicine was in part preordained: "By the time I was fourteen, it was 'understood' that I was going to be a doctor. My mother and father were both physicians, and so were my two eldest brothers."[2]

Sacks obtained his medical degree from the University of Oxford in England. One of his brothers was diagnosed at an early age with schizophrenia,* a mental disorder that causes people to interpret reality in a very subjective fashion; his subsequent treatment influenced Sacks to leave England. He recalls in his memoir:"When I left England on my twenty-seventh birthday, it was, among many other reasons, partly to get away from my tragic, hopeless, mismanaged brother."[3] His brother's illness and experience also influenced his own studies, and he attributes his migration also as "an attempt to explore schizophrenia and allied brain-mind disorders in my own patients and in my own way."[4] He settled first in the Canadian city of Montreal before moving to the United States, where he completed his postgraduate training. He eventually relocated to New York, where he began his long association with New York University in 1966.

Sacks's early personal experiences with neurological conditions and the mind shaped his later works. For instance, he suffered from prosopagnosia,* a disorder that limited his ability to perceive and recognize faces. He later wrote of this condition in *The Man Who Mistook his Wife.* He also experimented with drugs in his early career. Recalling his 20s and 30s he wrote: "I was professionally interested in brain states, mind states, of all sorts, not least those induced or modified by drugs … and I longed to experience these myself."[5] In his memoir, he further rationalized this drug use: "Such experiences, I thought, might help me understand what some of my patients were going through."[6] Some of these drug-induced states became topics in his later works. In fact one case study in the book details a patient who, after a mania* induced by an excess of stimulant drugs "developed an extraordinary sense of smell."[7] He later admitted that "this story was really about my own experience."[8]

Author's Background

Another reason Sacks left England involved the clash he saw between his personality and English culture. In an interview he recalled this sentiment: "I thought of British society as rigid and hierarchical. You were classified as soon as you opened your mouth. I imagined America would be socially and culturally and morally spacious."[9]

Sacks sought a more permissive lifestyle and found it during the 1960s in San Francisco and Los Angeles, where he completed his residency and medical fellowships in local hospitals. "During the week, I would avoid drugs [while at the hospital] … but on the weekends I often experimented with drugs."[10] Writing of the hallucinogenic drugs in his 2013 book *Hallucinations*, he explains:"On the West Coast [of the US] in the early nineteen-sixties, LSD* and morning-glory seeds* were readily available, so I sampled those."[11] In drugs, Sacks found a way to explore and extend his consciousness*—his awareness of himself and his place in the world—and his mind. And although he eventually broke from his drug use, citing the damage it caused him, he credits these experiences with providing epiphanies—sudden, striking insights—that shaped his life as a physician and author. For instance, he attributed to a drug-induced mania the realization that he should write case studies* in the manner of the nineteenth-century medical writer Edward Liveing:* "When I came down, I retained a sense of illumination and insight ... I had a sense of resolution, too, that I was indeed equipped to write a Liveing-like book, that perhaps I could be the Liveing of our time."[12]

NOTES

1   David Wallace-Wells, "A Brain With a Heart," *New York Magazine*, November 4, 2012, accessed September 22, 2015, http://nymag.com/news/features/oliver-sacks-2012-11/.

2   Oliver Sacks, *On the Move: A Life* (New York: Alfred A. Knopf, 2015), 12.

3   Sacks, *On the Move*, 65.

4   Sacks, *On the Move*, 65.

5   Sacks, *On the Move*, 115.

6   Sacks, *On the Move*, 115.

7   Sacks, *On the Move*, 252.

8   Sacks, *On the Move*, 252.

9   Lisa Burrell, "Life's Work: Oliver Sacks," *Harvard Business Review*, November 2010, accessed August 18, 2015, https://hbr.org/2010/11/lifes-work-oliver-sacks.

10 Oliver Sacks, "Altered States: Self-experiments in Chemistry," *The New Yorker*, August 27, 2012, accessed August 18, 2015, http://www.newyorker.com/magazine/2012/08/27/altered-states-3.

11 Oliver Sacks, *Hallucinations*, (New York: Vintage Books, 2013), 106.

12 Sacks, *Hallucinations*, 119.

MODULE 2
ACADEMIC CONTEXT

KEY POINTS

- The primary concerns of the medical community are accurate and effective diagnosis and treatment of patients.

- Technological advances in the 1970s and 1980s helped usher in an evidence-based* approach to neurology* — diagnosis and treatment of disorders of the brain and nervous system founded on systematic research.

- Sacks was strongly influenced by the pioneering neurologist John Hughlings Jackson* and the Russian neuropsychologist* Alexander R. Luria;* the latter was instrumental in convincing him to consider patient case studies.*

The Work in its Context

When Oliver Sacks wrote *The Man Who Mistook His Wife for a Hat* in the early 1980s, Western approaches to neurology and medicine were dominated by clinical expertise* and evidence-based medicine. In fact, these two approaches still dominate today.

Clinical expertise typically refers to a physician* making judgments about patients' diagnoses and treatment courses based on training, intuition, and experiences with other patients and conditions. In the 1970s and 1980s, Geoff Norman,* a scholar noted for his work on the decision-making of practicing physicians, noted that medical educators assumed that a physician's ability to detect and accurately predict ailments "was apparently related strongly to content knowledge."[1] Around the same time, evidence-based medicine began to gain influence. In this approach, doctors rely on empirical evidence (that is, evidence verifiable by observation), typically from studies conducted

> ❝ The scientific and the romantic in such realms cry out to come together—Luria liked to speak here of 'romantic science.'❞
>
> Oliver Sacks, *The Man Who Mistook His Wife for a Hat*

to determine if a particular medicine or treatment is safe and effective, to inform decision-making in diagnosis and treatment. The promotion of evidence-based medicine grew as medical researchers began to question the reliability of a physician's clinical reasoning alone.

In a paper of 1984, the US healthcare analyst David M. Eddy,* an early proponent of the method, summarized these concerns: "Uncertainty, biases, errors, and differences of opinions, motives, and values weaken every link in the chain that connects a patient's actual condition to the selection of a diagnostic test or treatment."[2] And yet both these approaches tend to focus on the physician's knowledge base—their experiences with prior patients (clinical expertise) or best practices based on the current research findings (evidence-based medicine).

These approaches, then, tend not to focus on the patient's inner and outer experiences or their personal history—factors that would form the heart of Sacks's written work.

Overview of the Field

Neurologists benefited from many research and technological breakthroughs in the 1970s. A review of the history of the field through the twentieth century noted that "the most significant scientific discovery of this decade was in the field of neuroimaging."[3] These advances provided doctors with visuals of a patient's brain activity, which they could then utilize in making diagnoses. "The next decade saw widespread clinical application of this [imaging] technique to the diagnosis of [damage or abnormalities of the brain]."[4]

It was also around this time that the neuroscientists Hanna Damasio* and Antonio Damasio* applied these techniques to find localized regions of the brain associated with certain neurological conditions. In *The Man Who Mistook His Wife* Sacks credits the pair with conducting "the most important studies of … agnosias* [the inability to interpret sensations, and hence to recognize things] and of visual processing in general."[5] Combined with the earlier work of Canadian neurosurgeon Wilder Penfield,* who uncovered brain regions associated with sensory and motor control,* neurology greatly advanced its knowledge of brain structure and function.

As neurologists gained the ability to visualize some brain activity, the evidence-based approach flourished. Yet although the neurologists possessed stronger tools to detect and diagnose conditions, the advances threatened to weaken the influence of clinical expertise in the physician's decision-making process. The neuroimaging pioneer William H. Oldendorf,* hoping to prepare neurologists for coming changes, wrote in 1975 that advanced brain-scanning techniques were "going to threaten the clinical neurological world" and were "beginning to fulfill much of the function of a neurological consultation."[6]

Academic Influences

Professionally and intellectually, Oliver Sacks was guided and mentored by Alexander R. Luria, a Russian neuropsychologist—a specialist in the ways brain injuries or illnesses affect behavior—whose works Sacks deemed "the greatest neurological treasure of our time, for both thought and case description."[7]

Luria wished for a more humane and less impersonal neurology, writing texts that detailed his most interesting patients in novel form. He focused on both their biographical and personal histories and their experiences of the disorder, before incorporating his own scientific explanations. Luria did not reject an evidence-based approach, though;

he hoped instead for a restoration of narrative case studies as a tool for writing about and understanding neurology. In his 1972 text *The Man with a Shattered World*, Luria wrote:"The power to describe, which was so common to the great nineteenth-century neurologists and psychiatrists, is almost gone now ... It must be revived."[8] And so Sacks took up the challenge; he often corresponded with Luria, and included some of these communications in *The Man Who Mistook His Wife for a Hat*. In the book, Sacks wrote of his influence: "Luria thought a science of this kind would be best introduced by a story ... In one of his last letters to me he wrote: 'Publish such [patient] histories, even if they are just sketches. It is a realm of great wonder.'"[9]

Sacks also cites the impact of the English neurologist John Hughlings Jackson, whom he considered "the founder of neurology as a science."[10] Jackson was part of a school of thought that viewed the brain as mechanical and analogous to a computer. While considering the field of neurology over-reliant on the analogy, Sacks notes that there was a degree of nuance in his work; "the Hughlings Jackson who wrote of 'dreamy states' and 'reminiscence,*'" he wrote, "was very different from the Jackson who saw all thought as [mathematical logic]. The former was a poet, the latter a logician, and yet they are one and the same man."[11]

NOTES

1   Geoffrey Norman, "Research in Clinical Reasoning: Past History and Current Trends," *Medical Education* 39, no. 4 (2005): 420.

2   David M. Eddy, "Variations in Physician Practice: The Role of Uncertainty," *Health Affairs* 3, no. 2 (1984): 75.

3   Kenneth Tyler et al., "Part 2: History of 20th-Century Neurology: Decade by Decade," *Annals of Neurology* 53, no. S4 (2003): S38.

4   Tyler et al., "Decade by Decade," S39.

5   Oliver Sacks, *The Man Who Mistook His Wife for a Hat and Other Clinical Tales* (New York: Touchstone, 1998), 14.

6   The American Society of Neuroimaging, "History of Neuroimaging," accessed August 18, 2015, http://www.asnweb.org/i4a/pages/index. cfm?pageid=3334.

7   Sacks, *The Man Who Mistook His Wife*, 235.

8   Alexander R. Luria, *The Man With a Shattered World: The History of a Brain Wound* (Cambridge: Harvard University Press, 1972), vii.

9   Sacks, *The Man Who Mistook His Wife*, 5–6.

10 Sacks, *The Man Who Mistook His Wife*, 235.

11 Sacks, *The Man Who Mistook His Wife*, 234.

MODULE 3
THE PROBLEM

KEY POINTS

- In the 1980s, physicians and medical researchers were concerned with the proper balance of two approaches: clinical expertise,* an approach founded on the accumulated knowledge and skill of the individual clinician, and evidence-based medicine,* an approach founded on the accumulation of rigorous research.

- The Russian neuropsychologist* Alexander R. Luria,* Sacks's mentor, argued for a more patient-centered* approach, emphasizing the patient's particular history, condition, and experience.

- Following Luria, Oliver Sacks pushed a patient-centered approach to neurology and medicine.

Core Question

In *The Man Who Mistook His Wife for a Hat*, Oliver Sacks addressed how neurologists interacted with and treated patients.

Typically, physicians seek to provide patients with quality, effective treatment, which includes providing an accurate diagnosis and manageable, effective treatment options. Different methods have been used to achieve this goal. In the 1980s, these approaches mostly combined clinical expertise and evidence–based medicine. But these are broad approaches at best: in a 1984 paper, the healthcare analyst David M. Eddy* cautioned of "the alarming variations [in approaches] we observe in actual practice."[1]

Beyond these swings, research of the time debunked some assumptions of what made for quality care. For instance, the prevailing belief in the 1970s and early 1980s was that physicians

> ❝ The tradition of richly human clinical tales reached a high point in the nineteenth century, and then declined, with the advent of an impersonal neurological science. ❞
>
> Oliver Sacks, *The Man Who Mistook His Wife for a Hat*

with better memory of prior patients—their conditions and treatment outcomes—had higher levels of clinical expertise and therefore provided better care. But research accumulated in the 1980s dismissed this assumption, as noted by the medical scholar Geoff Norman* in summarizing findings from this period: "In medicine, there is little gain from gathering and remembering extensive amounts of patient data, consequently thoroughness is a poor index of expertise."[2]

It was unclear, then, what represented the best balance of approaches to provide quality patient care. Into this void stepped Sacks, who was poised to provide his own approach—which differed in some key aspects to the prevailing ideas that had taken hold in neurology.

The Participants

Alexander R. Luria also fell somewhat outside the clinical expertise and evidence-based medicine approaches, as evidenced in a correspondence with Sacks about treating a patient with memory loss: "A man does not consist of memory alone. He has feeling, will, sensibility, moral being ... It is here ... you may touch him, and see a profound change."[3]

In his 1968 text *The Mind of a Mnenomist*, which detailed the experience of a single patient with extraordinary memory, Luria described himself as unlike other neuropsychologists because he "did not confine himself to measuring the capacity and stability of the subject's memory."[4] Instead, he was far more concerned with "what effect does a remarkable capacity for memory have on other major aspects of personality ... [and] ... what changes occur in a person's inner world."[5]

Luria, then, argued for a more rounded and complete view of the patient than was popular at the time Sacks wrote *The Man Who Mistook His Wife for a Hat*. He argued that a thoughtful physician was concerned with how a condition alters "the activity of the entire organism, thus giving rise to the total picture of disease."[6] Sacks adopted this mindset; as he writes: "I think a physician should be seen as a therapist. A good physiotherapist should have some idea of the patient's psyche."[7]

A leading voice for change in how physicians approached their decision-making was Eddy, who warned in 1984 that "some of the uncertainty and the resulting variations in practice patterns that exist are unavoidable, but much of the uncertainty can be managed far better than is done now."[8] Eddy developed his own set of recommendations for practicing medicine, centered mostly on both the clinical expertise and evidence-based medicine approaches. For instance, he called for explicit standards and policies for determining the best practices among physicians and for more funding for the study of conditions. These suggestions, however, focused on the medical community itself—without taking into consideration the very patients it served.

The Contemporary Debate

Sacks did not directly participate in the broader debate over how to provide the best medical treatment. He did not write in response to Eddy or others who pushed for research into the most effective practices. But it did concern him that doctors had begun to view patients impersonally. In an early book published in 1973, *Awakenings*, Sacks was clear about this issue, writing that, "in present-day medicine ... there is an almost exclusively technical or mechanical emphasis, which has led to immense advances, but also to intellectual regression, and a lack of proper attention to the full needs and feelings of patients."[9] Sacks also corresponded during this period with Luria, who promoted a similar approach.

Yet the two men had few if any vocal or powerful supporters. Those debating best practices for medical decision-making did not highlight the patient-centered approaches Luria and Sacks championed. Instead, they focused on reducing uncertainty and improving accuracy in assessing illness—and this often meant increasing rigorous research on diseases, conditions, drugs, and treatments. Eddy, however, did make recommendations involving patients; for example, he suggested that physicians be more forthcoming when they faced uncertainty about a diagnosis or treatment, and also noted that "patients can push the process by asking questions."[10]

Though this was nowhere near the patient-centered approach of Luria, Sacks and others, which framed the patient's requirements in narrative terms, it did include the person seeking treatment as part of the decision-making framework—or at least more so than the dominant clinical expertise and evidence-based approaches had done in the past.

NOTES

1   David M. Eddy, "Variations in Physician Practice: The Role of Uncertainty," *Health Affairs* 3, no. 2 (1984): 75.

2   Geoffrey Norman, "Research in Clinical Reasoning: Past History and Current Trends," *Medical Education* 39, no. 4 (2005): 420.

3   Oliver Sacks, *The Man Who Mistook His Wife for a Hat and Other Clinical Tales* (New York: Touchstone, 1998), 31.

4   Alexander R. Luria, *The Mind of a Mnemonist: A Little Book About a Vast Memory*, trans. Lynn Solotaroff (New York: Basic Books, 1987), 4.

5   Luria, *The Mind of a Mnemonist*, 4.

6   Luria, *The Mind of a Mnemonist*, 5.

7   Lisa Burrell, "Life's Work: Oliver Sacks," *Harvard Business Review*,
    November 2010, accessed August 18, 2015, https://hbr.org/2010/11/lifes-
    work-oliver-sacks.

8   Eddy, "The Role of Uncertainty," 88.

9   Oliver Sacks, *Awakenings* (New York: Vintage Books, 1990), xviii.

10 Eddy, "The Role of Uncertainty," 88.

MODULE 4
THE AUTHOR'S CONTRIBUTION

KEY POINTS

- Oliver Sacks believed the subjective experiences of patients—the experiences unique to them—provided valuable insights that could improve their care.

- Sacks used case studies*—detailed accounts of a single patient's condition and treatment—framed as narratives to explore his patients' conditions and experiences.

- Sacks adopted the approaches of the neuropsychologist Alexander R. Luria* and the pioneering psychoanalyst* Sigmund Freud* in becoming more receptive to his patients' experiences.

Author's Aims

In *The Man Who Mistook His Wife for a Hat*, Oliver Sacks hoped to "restore the human subject at the center"[1] of the case history, a genre used in neurology* to describe the course of disorders of the brain and nervous system by focusing not only on the symptoms but also on the patients' subjective experiences. Though writing narrative case studies was once popular in neurology, it had fallen out of favor among its practitioners, with the exception of Alexander R. Luria. Sacks aimed to examine neurological disorders from multiple points of view in order to understand what they meant for the patients and their existence, referring to his approach as the "neurology of identity."[2]

Sacks also wished to focus attention on neurological conditions that, in his view, had previously been overlooked by the field and the public. He aimed to detail neurological conditions originating from the right hemisphere* of the brain and noted in *The Man Who Mistook*

> ❝ Constantly my patients drive me to question, and constantly my questions drive me to patients. ❞
>
> Oliver Sacks, *The Man Who Mistook His Wife for a Hat*

His Wife that this "was a whole realm which Luria had not touched."[3] In fact, few physicians until that point had written of right-hemisphere conditions.

In addition Sacks felt that the mainstream of the field had equated neurological disorder with the loss of a function, and he sought to shed light on conditions that did not involve loss or deficit. Stating his interests in *The Man Who Mistook His Wife*, Sacks wrote, "disorders may be of many kinds—and may arise from excesses, no less than impairments, of function—and it seems reasonable to consider these two categories separately."[4] By focusing on conditions and approaches often neglected by much of the neurological community, Sacks was going against the grain.

Approach

The Man Who Mistook His Wife for a Hat comprises 24 case histories that Sacks transformed into short tales examining the influence of rare neurological disorders on the identities and lives of affected people. Sacks's focus on how these people struggled to incorporate their disorder into daily existence was particularly unusual. He declared that he was as interested in people as in diseases, writing in the text's preface: "I am equally, if inadequately, a theorist and dramatist, am equally drawn to the scientific and the romantic, and continually see both in the human condition."[5]

Indeed, he writes each story by applying many conventions associated with drama: he develops each patient's character, including snapshots of his or her daily life; he describes how the patients fought to manage their disorder, their identity, and their social lives; and he concludes each story with a postscript of how the patient fared after some time had passed following the initial treatment. Relating his approach to that of classical literature and myth, Sacks writes: "Classical fables have archetypal figures—heroes, victims, martyrs, warriors. Neurological patients are all of these—and in the strange tales told here they are also something more."[6]

This approach also enabled Sacks to market the text for a broader audience, rather than only the medical community. Sacks did not intend *The Man Who Mistook His Wife* to present a systematic examination of neurological disorders—and as a result, shunned neurological jargon and the need to inundate readers with comprehensive data and evidence.

Contribution in Context

Although Sacks's narrative case study approach was unique in neurology of the mid 1980s, it draws on both his earlier work and the work of thinkers who influenced him. Sacks's second book, *Awakenings* (1973), was his first attempt to merge a scientific case study with a literary narrative. In it, he focuses on patients suffering from encephalitis lethargica* (a neurological disorder marked by extreme feelings of tiredness and weakness in the body) who find a temporary cure with a new drug treatment. In *Awakenings*, Sacks identifies his approach as having been based on the received ideas of Luria: "In our own, technological age, there has often been a downgrading of case-history as being 'unscientific.'"[7] But, Sacks continued, "[with] Luria, there has been a reconsideration of narrative as an indispensable scientific tool."[8]

Luria's prior works were an obvious influence on *The Man Who Mistook His Wife*; Sacks repeatedly references Luria's approaches throughout the book. Luria had aimed to merge patients' subjective experiences with the neurological descriptions of disorders affecting them, an approach Luria referred to as "romantic science."[9] Sacks held this term—and this concept—in high regard.

Sacks also draws from psychologists, especially those of the early twentieth century, whose field was more traditionally concerned with the subjective experiences of patients. He refers in particular to Sigmund Freud, who suggested that when assessing patients, physicians "simply listen, and not bother about whether he [the physician] is keeping anything in mind."[10] Yet as Sacks attempted to add key aspects of psychology to neurology—that is, the examination of a patient's feelings and experiences—he prompted his colleagues to keep something in mind: how they could consider new approaches to treat those in their care.

NOTES

1   Oliver Sacks, *The Man Who Mistook His Wife for a Hat and Other Clinical Tales* (New York: Touchstone, 1998), VIII.

2   Sacks, *The Man Who Mistook His Wife*, X.

3   Sacks, *The Man Who Mistook His Wife*, 4.

4   Sacks, *The Man Who Mistook His Wife*, 6.

5   Sacks, *The Man Who Mistook His Wife*, VII.

6   Sacks, *The Man Who Mistook His Wife*, IX.

7   Oliver Sacks, *Awakenings* (New York: Vintage Books, 1990), 229.

8   Sacks, *Awakenings*, 229.

9   Alexander R. Luria, *The Mind of a Mnemonist: A Little Book About a Vast Memory*, trans. Lynn Solotaroff (New York: Basic Books, 1987), XIII.

10 Sigmund Freud, *Recommendations to Physicians Practising Psycho-Analysis* (London: The Hogarth Press, 1912), 111–12.

SECTION 2
IDEAS

MODULE 5
MAIN IDEAS

KEY POINTS

- Oliver Sacks stressed that neurological disorders*— disorders of the nervous system and brain—affect patients' sense of identity, and urged neurologists* to consider this when treating patients.

- Neurological disorders can destroy patients' sense of self just as readily as their memory, vision, or motor control.

- The 24 case studies* Sacks discusses describe the neurological conditions of his former patients.

Key Themes

In *The Man Who Mistook His Wife for a Hat* Oliver Sacks examines the relationship between neurological disorders and the subjective experiences of those who suffer from them. Sacks noted that his patients, in addition to the neurological and physical challenges associated with their disorders, often struggled to make sense of self and identity.

Sacks wished to highlight this struggle, which he argued is caused by the inevitable effects of the neurological disorder on patients' identity, writing: "There is always a reaction, on the part of the affected organism or individual, to restore, to replace, to compensate for and to preserve its identity, however strange the means may be."[1]

Indeed, a key theme throughout the text involves coping: Sacks details how his patients try to manage both their disorder and altered sense of self.

As a second theme, Sacks offers a critique of neurology as a field that had forgotten the influence of disorders on a patient's identity. Sacks was concerned that neurology had become overly reliant on the

> **❝ The study of disease and of identity cannot be disjoined. ❞**
> Oliver Sacks, *The Man Who Mistook His Wife for a Hat*

widely accepted analogy of the brain as a computer. To be sure, he did not disavow it, writing that "the brain is a machine and a computer—everything in classical neurology is correct."[2] But he believed that the field had lost sight of the costs paid by those with neurological disorders: interpersonal, psychological, and existential—that is, related to the fact of their very existence.

He writes that "our mental processes, which constitute our being and life, are not just abstract and mechanical, but personal, as well—and, as such, involve not just classifying and categorizing, but continual judging and feeling also."[3] The abilities to judge and feel, Sacks argued, were staples of human identity—both threatened and altered in his patients.

Exploring the Ideas

In service of the first theme, Sacks focused on patients' experience, at times recalling their own words, while at other times providing his own impressions and analogies. For instance, in one case study Sacks discusses a patient, Ray, who has Tourette's syndrome,* a motor-impulse disorder—that is, a disorder that expresses itself in irresistible impulses to move—that typically results in tics, grimaces, and uncontrolled vocal noises. Sacks reported that Ray seemed unprepared for treatment and at times appeared resigned and even attached to his tics. "'Suppose you could take away the tics,' [Ray] said. 'What would be left? I consist of tics—there is nothing else.'"[4]

This exchange highlighted how, even as Ray struggled with his identity, his Tourette's was a large part of that identity. Sacks concluded that Ray "could not imagine life without Tourette's, nor was he sure he would care for it."[5]

In response, Sacks realized that he needed to show Ray the value of a life unconstrained by the syndrome, and encourage him to imagine a positive identity that did not include the symptoms that had come to define him. Sacks then spent three months with Ray examining "the role and economic importance of Tourette's to him, and how he might get on without these."[6] After these mental explorations Sacks put Ray back on medication, and this time Ray proved more receptive.

Sacks also considered external circumstances that affected his patients' attempts to cope. He believed that this fuller view of the disorder was vital.

Sacks reprints his correspondences with Alexander R. Luria,* who often coached him on diagnoses and treatments. In one such communication, Luria explained that at times, when little can be accomplished neurologically, much could be done psychologically. In one example, when Sacks sought advice on a patient with severe memory loss, Luria advised: "Neuropsychologically,* there is little or nothing you can do; but in the realm of the Individual, there may be much you can do."[7] Sacks passed this message on to his colleagues—that they needed to consider and address how neurological disorders affected their patients' identities.

Language and Expression

The 24 brief case studies in *The Man Who Mistook His Wife* each describe a patient or patients and their neurological condition. This typically involves cases in New York City during the 1970s and 1980s, when Sacks served as an expert neurologist. Through the case study format, Sacks details interactions that range from initial meetings and diagnoses to his attempts at treatment, before he concludes with a report on the patient's progress. This approach serves to supply the reader with a more engaging view into the patient's experience, showing how each person is affected by his or her condition over the course of months and years.

Throughout, Sacks includes medical terms and conditions that describe his patients. At times his writing includes tangential discussions of case studies popular in the field, and in these instances he often fails to define these terms—a sign that Sacks may be writing for the moment to an audience of medical colleagues. But when he details one of his patient's experiences, he does explain the medical jargon and typically relies on several methods to do so.

Beyond including definitions that detail the brain areas affected and describing physical and psychological symptoms, he also relies on metaphors and the patient's voice. For instance, in the case study of Tourette's syndrome, Sacks quotes a subjective description; "'I have too much energy,' one Tourette's patient said. 'Everything is too bright, too powerful, too much. It is a feverish energy, a morbid brilliance.'"[8]

In his use of metaphors, Sacks references literature, art, and music. For instance, he viewed his patient Dr. P's work as reflective of mental deterioration, seeing his later output as having "an almost Picasso*-like power to see, and equally depict, those abstract organizations embedded in, and normally lost in, the concrete …Though in the final pictures, I feared, there was only chaos and agnosia."*[9]

NOTES

1   Oliver Sacks, *The Man Who Mistook His Wife For a Hat and Other Clinical Tales* (New York: Touchstone, 1998), 8.

2   Sacks, *The Man Who Mistook His Wife*, 20.

3   Sacks, *The Man Who Mistook His Wife*, 20.

4   Sacks, *The Man Who Mistook His Wife*, 82.

5   Sacks, *The Man Who Mistook His Wife*, 82.

6   Sacks, *The Man Who Mistook His Wife*, 82.

7   Sacks, *The Man Who Mistook His Wife*, 32.

8   Sacks, *The Man Who Mistook His Wife*, 75.

9   Sacks, *The Man Who Mistook His Wife*, 18.

MODULE 6
SECONDARY IDEAS

KEY POINTS

- Oliver Sacks argued that neurology* focused too much on conditions originating from the left hemisphere* of the brain and those that entailed a "deficit"—a loss of function—of some kind.

- Sacks detailed several neurological conditions that originated from the right hemisphere* and did not involve any such loss.

- Although Sacks's desire to establish a "neurology of identity" was largely overlooked, the idea has recently sparked renewed interest.

Other Ideas

Oliver Sacks's *The Man Who Mistook His Wife for a Hat* contains two related secondary ideas. First, Sacks argues that neurological conditions are not simply a question of a deficit in some ability or capacity. Second, he focuses on states that originated from the brain's right hemisphere.

To demonstrate the wide range of effects, Sacks identifies four types of condition:

- *Losses* lead to a disappearance (a "deficit") in some function.
- *Excesses* lead to a "superabundance of function,"[1] such as seen in the irresistible tics and exclamations of people suffering from Tourette's syndrome.*
- *Transports* lead to dreamlike experiences of nostalgia or reminiscences of an earlier memory; one instance Sacks details involves seizures*—sudden surges in electrical activity in the temporal lobe* (a part of the brain involved with functions associated with sound), which can cause a patient to hear music in the mind.

> ❝ It is, then, less deficits, in the traditional sense, which have engaged my interest than neurological disorders affecting the self. ❞
>
> Oliver Sacks, *The Man Who Mistook His Wife for a Hat*

- *The World of the Simple* is a phrase Sacks uses in reference to patients with extreme mental deficits, such as from intellectual disability.

Beyond these distinctions, Sacks also focuses on right-hemisphere neurological conditions.

Both of these secondary ideas relate to one of Sacks's main thrusts in that they critique classical neurology. Writing that the field of neurology's "favorite word is 'deficit,'"[2] and that "the entire history of neurology and neuropsychology* can be seen as a history of the investigation of the left hemisphere,"[3] he argues that neurologists fixated on conditions that involved deficits, particularly those with origins in the left hemisphere of the brain.

Exploring the Ideas

Sacks takes issue with neurology's narrow view of disorders, and believes the field relied too much on a model according to which the brain is a mechanical or computerized organ. He holds that this belief has led neurologists to consider only an all-or-nothing brain functioning: "Either the function (like a capacitor or fuse) is normal—or it is defective or faulty: what other possibility is there for a mechanistic neurology, which is essentially a system of capacities and connections?"[4]

Sacks feels that such a conceptualization kept neurologists from seeing a nuanced or broader range of possible conditions. In discussing the limitations of a deficit-focus approach to neurology, Sacks writes:

"What then of the opposite—an excess or superabundance of function? Neurology has no word for this—because it has no concept. A function, or functional system, works—or it does not: these are the only possibilities it allows."[5]

Tourette's syndrome, an over-excitation of the motor impulses*— impulses that lead to physical movement—is one such condition that Sacks describes as an excess.

Sacks categorizes another overlooked set of conditions as "transports," writing: "For it never occurs to us [neurologists] at first that a vision might be 'medical'; and if an organic basis is suspected or found, this may be felt to 'devalue' the vision (though, of course, it does not—values, valuations, have nothing to do with etiology*)."[6] He writes of a patient, Ms. O'C, whose temporal lobe seizures caused her to hear music that reminded her of her childhood; Ms. O'C was grateful for these transports and the condition that caused them. Sacks concludes that Ms. O'C could not be suffering from a dysfunction, and that her case offered evidence that neurological conditions existed that should not be considered as the cause of some deficit.

Sacks also questions neurology's focus on the brain's left hemisphere, providing two reasons for this imbalance in medical research. "One important reason for the neglect of the right, or 'minor,' hemisphere, as it has always been called, is that while it is easy to demonstrate the effects of variously located lesions [abnormalities] on the left side, the corresponding syndromes of the right hemisphere are much less distinct."[7] Not only were right-hemisphere conditions more difficult to study and diagnose, but they were also less interesting to neurologists. According to Sacks, the right hemisphere "was presumed, usually contemptuously, to be more 'primitive' than the left, the latter being seen as the unique flower of human evolution."[8]

Overlooked

Sacks is adamant that neurologists had an imperative to consider how neurological conditions affect a patient's sense of self and identity. Though the field was eventually to address this concern, Sacks also offers a specific method, which went overlooked, toward addressing it.

He proposed a new framework he called the "neurology of identity,"[9] where examining patient identities would play an essential role in the diagnostic process when determining the physical manifestations of neurological disorders. Sacks proposes that such a framework would blend neurology, psychology, and the case study* approach; for the field to "restore the human subject at the center— the suffering, afflicted, fighting, human subject—we must deepen a case history to a narrative or tale; only then do we have a 'who' as well as a 'what,' a real person, a patient, in relation to disease—in relation to the physical," he writes.[10]

Sacks's "neurology of identity" did not develop into a prime framework for neurologists, however. As he notes, abstract psychological or narrative constructs such as identity were, at least at the time of his book, outside the field's scope, meaning that a foundational restructuring was unlikely.

That said, the medical field has shown increasing interest of late in patients' personal concerns. This can be seen in the rising prominence of narrative medicine,* which stresses the importance of doctors listening to their patients' subjective concerns and considering these when planning treatment. The American physician Rita Charon,* a leading proponent of this approach, expresses concerns similar to those of Sacks. In a 2001 article she wrote: "The effective practice of medicine requires narrative competence, that is, the ability to acknowledge, absorb, interpret, and act on the stories and plights of others."[11]

NOTES

1 Oliver Sacks, *The Man Who Mistook His Wife For a Hat and Other Clinical Tales* (New York: Touchstone, 1998), 80.

2 Sacks, *The Man Who Mistook His Wife*, 3.

3 Sacks, *The Man Who Mistook His Wife*, 4.

4 Sacks, *The Man Who Mistook His Wife*, 80.

5 Sacks, *The Man Who Mistook His Wife*, 80.

6 Sacks, *The Man Who Mistook His Wife*, 123.

7 Sacks, *The Man Who Mistook His Wife*, 4.

8 Sacks, *The Man Who Mistook His Wife*, 4.

9 Sacks, *The Man Who Mistook His Wife*, VIII.

10 Sacks, *The Man Who Mistook His Wife*, VIII.

11 Rita Charon, "Narrative Medicine: A Model for Empathy, Reflection, Profession, and Trust," *Journal of the American Medical Association* 286, no. 15 (2001): 1897.

MODULE 7
ACHIEVEMENT

KEY POINTS

- In *The Man Who Mistook His Wife for a Hat*, Oliver Sacks artistically conveys the subjective experiences of his patients.

- Works of popular science* — books discussing scientific matters written for a general audience — gained interest with the public in the 1980s.

- Sacks relies on the experiences of a few similar patients and on current neurological diagnoses that some outside the medical community would not accept.

Assessing the Argument

With *The Man Who Mistook His Wife for a Hat,* Oliver Sacks set out to provide rich, biographical, and narrative case studies* of his patients—and in this regard he succeeded. A 1986 *New York Times* review concluded that "[Sacks] recounts these [patients'] histories with the lucidity and power of a gifted short-story writer."[1] The review also noted that "Oliver Sacks has a decidedly original approach to these problems,"[2] although Sacks himself might contend that he was simply reviving the methodology of Alexander R. Luria* and others.

Meanwhile, those in the scientific community expressed similar sentiments. A 1985 review in the respected science journal *Nature* praised Sacks's writing, suggesting that the book "deserves to be widely read whether for its message, or as an easy introduction to neurological symptoms, or simply as a collection of moving tales."[3]

Sacks also hoped such narratives would pique the interest of neurologists—and move them to adopt more patient-centered*

> ❝ The best science writing, such as the remarkable case studies in *The Man Who Mistook His Wife for a Hat* by Oliver Sacks, teaches us narrative. ❞
> Roald Hoffmann, "The Metaphor, Unchained"

practices—while making them receptive to hearing and documenting patients' stories when plotting a course of treatment. Here the scientific community expressed caution. The same reviewer in *Nature*, for instance, advised non-medical readers that Sacks oversimplified cases through dramatization:"The reader should, however, bring to it a little skepticism, for outside Sacks's clinic, things do not always fall out quite so pat."[4]

Yet in cases like this, scientific communities are generally and rightfully doubtful. And *The Man Who Mistook His Wife* admittedly presented a non-scientific telling of just two dozen patients and their experiences. Although the text could not pinpoint the precise role that patient-centered* narratives should play in physicians' routines, it is worth noting that no single text could achieve such a feat.

Achievement in Context

The Man Who Mistook His Wife succeeded as a work of popular science,* introducing neurological disorders to a general audience unfamiliar with neurology* and the rare conditions Sacks spotlights. Neurology in the 1980s represented a small specialty field in medicine; estimates showed there were fewer than 5,000 neurologists in the United States in 1980, with some claiming the field was understaffed. And few books in the field were previously available to the general public, or written in a literary, rather than a medical or academic, style.

In crafting a work of popular science, Sacks risked his credibility with fellow neurologists. One reviewer noted the difficulty Sacks faced with his early works such as *The Man Who Mistook His Wife*:"For much of the twentieth century, doctors and scientists who appealed to the public were derided by their peers, seen as popularizers who watered down knowledge and exploited patients."[5]

This viewpoint changed, however, around the time Sacks began writing. In a text discussing the increasing public exposure of scientists Declan Fahy,* a scholar noted for his analyses of science journalism, wrote: "Beginning in 1970, the amount of science reported in the media exploded."[6] As evidence, Fahy cited these developments: "In the United States, the 1970s and 1980s saw the creation of science sections in dozens of newspapers across the country, the launch of multiple glossy popular science magazines, and the inauguration of a new weekly television series—*Nova*—devoted to science."[7] Accordingly, the text benefitted from entering the public domain at a time when readers yearned for science literature—and works of neurology were still quite novel.

Limitations

The few patients discussed in *The Man Who Mistook His Wife* are a demographically similar bunch—that is, they come from much the same section of society. A few were well off enough to afford neurological consultation and treatment. All lived in New York City, where Sacks practiced medicine in the 1970s and 1980s. Sacks, however, also included historical case studies in the text as references, often reinterpreting these reports in a medical context. He explores, for instance, historical reports of religious visions, writing that "the religious literature of all ages is replete with descriptions of 'visions' ... [but] ... It is impossible to ascertain, in the vast majority of cases, whether the experience represents a hysterical or psychotic ecstasy, the effects of intoxication, or an epileptic or migrainous manifestation."[8]

He provides one instance that he believes offers enough historical documentation to venture a modern diagnosis: the case of Hildegard of Bingen,* a Christian saint and mystic who lived in the twelfth century and experienced multiple religious visions that she wrote down. Sacks discusses modern neurological explanations for these phenomena, arguing that they amounted to hallucinations* caused by migraine headaches. Sacks knew that many devout Christians (and perhaps Hildegard herself) would not share his interpretation—that what neurology labels as a disorder may not necessarily be perceived as such by the affected person or others who share a common set of religious beliefs.

Nevertheless, the US English scholar G. Thomas Couser* criticized Sacks's lack of consideration for culture. In his review of the work, he wrote: "Sacks is generally more concerned with the individual adaptations than with the process by which culture produces 'biological' norms."[9] In other words, Sacks details how people might cope with a disorder given their culture, as in the case of Hildegard. But he tends to ignore whether a culture deems a particular condition normal, instead considering all neurological disorders as abnormal.

NOTES

1   John C. Marshall, "In the Region of Lost Minds," *New York Times*, March 2, 1986, accessed September 22, 2015, https://www.nytimes.com/books/98/12/06/specials/sacks-mistook.html.

2   Marshall, "In the Region of Lost Minds."

3   Stuart Sutherland, "Review of Sacks, *The Man Who Mistook His Wife for a Hat*," *Nature* 318, no. 609 (1985): 19.

4   Sutherland, "Review of Sacks,"19.

5   Julia Belluz, "Why Oliver Sacks Was So Ambivalent About Becoming a Best-selling Author," *Vox*, July 17, 2015, accessed August 18, 2015, http://www.vox.com/2015/4/27/8503113/oliver-sacks-dr-oz.

6   Declan Kahy, *The New Celebrity Scientists: Out of the Lab and into the Limelight* (London: Rowman & Littlefield, 2015), 3.

7   Kahy, *New Celebrity Scientists*, 3–4.

8   Oliver Sacks, *The Man Who Mistook His Wife For a Hat and Other Clinical Tales* (New York: Touchstone, 1998), 161.

9   G. Thomas Couser, *Vulnerable Subjects: Ethics and Life Writing* (New York: Cornell University Press, 2004), 113.

MODULE 8
PLACE IN THE AUTHOR'S WORK

KEY POINTS

- Much of Oliver Sacks's prolific writing career was dedicated to presenting the personal stories of his patients.

- In his later works, Sacks continued to rely on approaches similar to those he used in *The Man Who Mistook His Wife for a Hat*—specifically narrative case studies* intended to portray patients' experiences.

- Sacks became a best-selling author, which vaulted him to the status of famous neurologist* and popular science* writer.

Positioning

In his fourth book, *The Man Who Mistook His Wife for a Hat,* Oliver Sacks extended many of the patient-centered* themes of identity found in his earlier works. G. Thomas Couser,* a scholar noted for his analysis of studies of disability, echoed this while reviewing Sacks's career work: "From early in his career [Sacks] has aspired to practice what he calls a 'romantic neurology,' by which he means a neurology that recovers the 'I' or the 'who' (the patient's subjectivity) form the 'it' or the 'what' (the physiological condition)."[1]

These themes particularly emerged in Sacks's second book, *Awakenings* (1973). Writing in 1990 of his motivations and the intent behind that work, Sacks discussed how only a presentation of case histories or biographies could convey the experiences of his patients in an effective and humane manner. He took this risk because "no 'orthodox' presentation, in terms of numbers, series, grading of effects, etc., could have conveyed the historical reality of the experience."[2]

> ❝ *The Man Who Mistook* would mark the beginning of another career, and a much more public one, as perhaps the unlikeliest ambassador for brain science. ❞
>
> David Wallace-Wells, "A Brain With a Heart"

Sacks published a total of 11 books; many included narrative case studies in which he provided insights, as best he could, into his patients' subjective worlds. His 1995 book *An Anthropologist on Mars*, for example, restates his support for this career-long theme: "The study of disease, for the physician, demands the study of identity, the inner worlds that patients, under the spur of illness, create."[3] But after *The Man Who Mistook His Wife*, he gradually adjusted his view of how the brain works—at least in regard to the localization of functions,* a theory that dated to the 1860s and held that different brain areas controlled different functioning. He wrote in his 2015 memoir of his early reliance on localization, saying that then his thinking "was still grounded in this model, in which the nervous system was largely conceived as fixed and invariant, with 'pre-dedicated' areas for every function."[4] Along with his colleagues, Sacks would later view many of the brain's functions as a result of interaction between several areas.

Integration

Sacks dedicated much of his career to providing personalized care and publishing thought-provoking texts that relied on narrative case studies.

Earlier in his career, he engaged more in medical research, most notably involving L-dopa,* a drug associated with the treatment of the progressive neurological condition Parkinson's Disease,* which helped some of the patients he discusses in *Awakenings*. Yet he never considered himself a researcher, writing in his memoir: "I felt that my research career as a whole was a failure and that I could never hope to be a research scientist."[5] His popular writings enjoyed increasing success, however, and retained similar themes over the course of almost five decades.

Aside from relying on narrative case studies as his way to convey patient experiences, he promoted the concepts of a "neurology of identity" (according to which the neurologist should deliberately consider patients' identity and their experience of their condition) and "romantic science" (a term, inherited by Sacks from his mentor Alexander R. Luria,* that describes an approach in which the patients' condition is understood in the light of their experience).

As his career progressed, Sacks found new means to achieve his goals. In his book *Musicophilia* (2007), for instance, Sacks explores the relationship between music and his patients' symptoms and treatment, as he considers "the scarcity of musical case histories."[6] And much in line with his broader aim to personalize and humanize his patients, he wrote of how neuroscientific* research on music risked becoming too mechanical: "There is now an enormous and rapidly growing body of work on the neural underpinnings of musical perception and imagery ... but there is always a certain danger that the simple art of observation may be lost ... and the richness of the human context ignored."[7]

In his later works, an additional theme gained increasing significance: discussions of consciousness* (very roughly, our awareness that we are alive, and of things external to us). This was the lynchpin of his 2013 book *Hallucinations*, in which Sacks detailed the meaning his patients ascribed to their visual and auditory hallucinations*—and that he did, as well. He described hallucinations as a "privileged state of consciousness"[8] in many other cultures, and expressed hope that Western cultures would one day view them the same way. But even here, Sacks relied on the narrative case study to explore how hallucinations affected patients' consciousness, self, and identity.

Significance

Though Sacks's earlier works embodied a theme and intent similar to *The Man Who Mistook His Wife*, they were overlooked—especially by the medical community. This disregard upset and confused Sacks, as he recalled in the preface of the 1990 reprint of *Awakenings*: "The 1973 publication of *Awakenings*, while attracting much general attention, met with the same cold reception from the profession as my articles had done earlier."[9] But in sharp contrast, *The Man Who Mistook His Wife* vaulted Sacks into the public discourse. In his 2015 memoir, he wrote of his surprise at the success of the work with the public. "The book's popularity grew," he noted, "and completely unexpectedly, it appeared on the *New York Times* bestseller list."[10]

Even more meaningful to him, he added, were "the letters which poured in, many from people who had themselves experienced problems which I had written about in *Hat*."[11] Yet at this point, Sacks became uneasy with his public status and the effect it had on his practice, recalling in his memoir that "with the sudden popularity of *[The Man Who Mistook His Wife]* ... I had entered the public sphere, whether I wanted it or not ... I had powers to help but also powers to harm."[12] In many ways, Sacks turned into the most visible neurologist in the eyes of the public—even though he did not represent the dominant mindset of his contemporaries.

NOTES

1 G. Thomas Couser, *Vulnerable Subjects: Ethics and Life Writing* (New York: Cornell University Press, 2004), 75.

2 Oliver Sacks, *Awakenings* (New York: Vintage Books, 1990), xxx.

3 Oliver Sacks, *An Anthropologist on Mars: Seven Paradoxical Tales* (New York: Knopf, 1995), 11.

4 Oliver Sacks, *On the Move: A Life* (New York: Alfred A. Knopf, 2015), 355.

5 Sacks, *On the Move*, 24.

6   Oliver Sacks, *Musicophilia: Tales of Music and the Brain* (New York: Vintage Books, 2007), xiv.

7   Sacks, *Musicophilia*, xiv.

8   Oliver Sacks, *Hallucinations* (New York: Vintage Books, 2012), xiv.

9   Sacks, *Awakenings*, xxxiv.

10 Sacks, *On the Move*, 254.

11 Sacks, *On the Move*, 255.

12 Sacks, *On the Move*, 256.

SECTION 3
IMPACT

MODULE 9
THE FIRST RESPONSES

KEY POINTS

- Though reaction to *The Man Who Mistook His Wife for a Hat* was generally positive, some believed that Sacks had manipulated his knowledge of neurology*—and worse, that he had exploited his patients.

- Most reviewers, however, enjoyed the writing, and Sacks had already written that his patients had approved of the inclusion of their stories.

- In later works Sacks would attempt more thorough methods for accessing and conveying his patients' experiences.

Criticism

Reviews of Oliver Sacks's *The Man Who Mistook His Wife for a Hat* were largely positive—particularly in the public sphere. Reviewers praised the text's readability, and the way in which Sacks conveyed both rare neurological conditions* and patient experiences to his audience. However, these literary reviews did contain some criticism. In his *New York Times* review, John C. Marshall found one aspect of the text "extremely annoying."[1] He questioned Sacks's tendency to play "naive about the neurological literature." In an otherwise positive review, Marshall wrote: "He would have us believe that an experienced neurologist could fail to have read anything about many of the standard syndromes of behavioral neurology until he had himself seen a particularly pure case of the condition in question."[2]

At first, *The Man Who Mistook His Wife* garnered little reaction from the medical community. Sacks recalled in his 2015 memoir *On*

> **❝ He recounts these [patient] histories with the lucidity and power of a gifted short-story writer. ❞**
>
> John C. Marshall, *In the Region of Lost Minds*

the Move that after the work's release, "by and large, the medical silence continued."[3] Yet Sacks certainly gained more visibility in the medical community, and so the silence itself amounted to criticism. Sacks gave an analysis in his memoir regarding the lack of reaction to the book: "My fellow neurologists … remained somewhat remote and dismissive … if one is popular, then ipso facto, one is not to be taken seriously."[4] But as he continued to publish, his colleagues would come to acknowledge and consider his ideas and fame.

Criticism would begin years later, with the most common revolving around the ethics of Sacks's portrayal of his patients. The political journalist Alexander Cockburn* was particularly bothered by Sacks's method, writing in 1993 that "Sacks is in the same business as the supermarket tabloids,"[5] and suggested that Sacks was allowing his readers to look voyeuristically "at the freaks."[6] Others later levied similar charges, concerned, like Cockburn, that Sacks was profiting from exploiting the conditions of his patients. More damning was the dismissal of disability-rights activist Tom Shakespeare,* who called Sacks "the man who mistook his patients for a literary career."[7]

Responses

Proponents of Sacks's method and work responded to the medical community's muted reaction by endorsing *The Man Who Mistook His Wife* and the idea of narrative medicine.* The US medical scholar Alan G. Wasserstein,* for example, was drawn to Sacks's use of narrative and his patient-centered* approach—so much so, that Wasserstein wrote that the entire medical field might benefit from Sacks's ideas. In a 1988 article reviewing Sacks's work, Wasserstein declared that medicine had lost the "empathy and humanness of the personal encounter."[8] And using similar terms as Sacks, he wrote that "mechanical medicine has … surrendered its consideration of the higher faculties. Sacks wants to restore the soul, the personal agent, to neurology and to medicine."[9]

As for the charge that Sacks presented watered-down science, not all agreed. The author Sandra Schor,* writing about effective science communication to the public, felt that "the writings of Oliver Sacks provide an excellent example of interdisciplinary thinking: he transforms the scientific case study* into an interpretive, humanistic essay—without 'translation' or simplification."[10]

While Sacks did not directly respond to Cockburn's accusations of exploitation, he noted that those under his care had approved him including their stories: "The patients … whose tales I tell here … permitted, even encouraged, me to write of their lives, in the hope that others might learn and understand, and, one day, perhaps be able to cure."[11]

Conflict and Consensus

Though not directly involved in a debate over *The Man Who Mistook His Wife*, Sacks did offer a reconsideration of the text, somewhat agreeing with the charge that the work was not as detailed and thorough as it could have been. He acknowledged as much in a 1989 interview, in which he said, "I partly have the feeling … that the *Hat* book is a sort of brilliant tour-de-force covering for some emptiness which a closer look discloses."[12] He continued, "I tend to apologize for the *Hat* book, saying 'That's just a little thing; go read *Awakenings*. That's the real one.'"[13] Sacks seemed to revisit this issue in his 1995 text, *An Anthropologist on Mars*. This later text shared both themes and structure with *The Man Who Mistook His Wife*—offering narrative case studies where he profiled the same or similar neurological conditions. But in *Anthropologist*, Sacks only included seven case studies, allowing himself to provide more detail both of his patients' conditions and of their histories and experiences. In *Anthropologist* Sacks declares: "The exploration of deeply altered selves and worlds is not one that can be fully made in a consulting room or office."[14] And thus Sacks completed much of his research by interviewing his patients in their homes and daily lives—a more thorough treatment than many of the cases in *The Man Who Mistook His Wife* received.

But in the end, Sacks stood by the work's major themes—and his narrative, case–study approach, coupled with the desire to have a more personalized neurology. And as these themes got the attention of some sympathetic members of the medical community, such as Wasserstein, Sacks continued publishing new books with similar themes. Thanks to his persistence, Sacks saw his ideas gain momentum and recognition in neurology and medicine.

The loud and disparaging criticisms Cockburn and others raised would also find supporters, however—especially since Sacks continued to publish similar works throughout the 1990s that relied on patient case studies.

NOTES

1   John C. Marshall, "In the Region of Lost Minds," *New York Times*, March 2, 1986, accessed August 18, 2015, https://www.nytimes.com/books/98/12/06/specials/sacks-mistook.html.

2   "In the Region of Lost Minds."

3   Oliver Sacks, *On the Move: A Life* (New York: Alfred A. Knopf, 2015), 256.

4   Sacks, *On the Move*, 256.

5   Alexander Cockburn, "Wonders in Barmy Land," *Nation* 256 (June 14, 1993): 822.

6   Cockburn, "Wonders in Barmy Land," 822.

7   Gregory Cowles, "Oliver Sacks, Neurologist Who Wrote About the Brain's Quirks, Dies at 82," *New York Times*, August 15, 2015, accessed September 23, 2015, http://www.nytimes.com/2015/08/31/science/oliver-sacks-dies-at-82-neurologist-and-author-explored-the-brains-quirks.html.

8   Alan G. Wasserstein, "Toward a Romantic Science: The Work of Oliver Sacks," *Annals of Internal Medicine* 109, no. 5 (1988): 440.

9   Wasserstein, "Toward a Romantic Science," 440.

10 Sandra Schor, "Writing across the Disciplines: Respecting the Untranslatable" (paper presented at the 38th Annual Meeting of the Conference on College Composition and Communication, Atlanta, GA, March 19–21, 1987).

11 Oliver Sacks, *The Man Who Mistook His Wife For a Hat and Other Clinical Tales* (New York: Touchstone, 1985), x.

12 Dale Flynn, Susan Palo, and Oliver Sacks, "An Interview with Oliver Sacks," *Writing on the Edge* 1, no. 1 (Fall, 1989): 105.

13 Flynn et al., "An Interview," 105.

14 Oliver Sacks, *An Anthropologist on Mars: Seven Paradoxical Tales* (New York: Knopf, 1995), 12.

MODULE 10
THE EVOLVING DEBATE

KEY POINTS

- Oliver Sacks's ideas would be referenced by the narrative medicine* movement, which sought to develop physicians'* patient care through a mix of training in literature and empathy.

- *The Man Who Mistook His Wife for a Hat* remains an early influence for the patient-centered* approach of narrative medicine.

- A respected example of quality popular science* writing, Sacks's book was one of the earliest to examine neurological conditions as more than the cause of some deficit—a deficiency in some mental or behavioral capacity.

Uses and Problems

The leading proponent of the ideas found in *The Man Who Mistook His Wife for a Hat* remained Oliver Sacks himself. Sacks published several other books from the 1980s until his death in 2015; while themes such as consciousness* became conspicuous in many, the ideas of *The Man Who Mistook His Wife* remained central as he continued to promote both narrative case studies* and a more romantic—that is, roughly, personalized—approach to patient–centered* care. These themes leapt to the fore in his 1995 book *An Anthropologist on Mars*, in which he wrote: "The realities of patients, the ways in which they and their brains construct their own worlds, cannot be comprehended wholly from the observation of behavior, from the outside."[1]

And further amplifying his call for a more holistic science,* he wrote, "In addition to the objective approach of the scientist, the naturalist, we must employ an intersubjective approach too."[2] The

> **"** Medicine has never been without narrative concerns, because, as an enterprise in which one human being extends help to another, it has always been grounded in life's intersubjective domain. **"**
>
> Rita Charon, *Narrative Medicine*

declarations gained weight as Sacks's position in the medical community became more prominent—and others, attracted to his ideas, incorporated them into what would be called narrative medicine. This broader movement sought to equip physicians better to reflect, and to acknowledge the personal stories of patients.

As Sacks's popularity grew, a few academics and writers again questioned the ethics of how he used his patients. As before, these centered on accusations that Sacks was more an exploiter than an innocent storyteller. Leonard Cassuto* wrote in a 2000 analysis of Sacks's body of work that this proved particularly true in his earlier works: "*The Man Who Mistook His Wife for a Hat* spotlights weird conditions rather than people."[3] While G. Thomas Couser,* a literature scholar known for his studies of disabilities, considered Sacks's ethics a worthy topic of discussion, he ultimately disagreed with Cassuto; in 2004, he wrote that it was "difficult to see how Sacks's patients are harmed or wronged as individuals by representation that is anonymous or consensual."[4] Sacks always referred to his patients by pseudonyms and acquired permission from the patients or their families before publishing their stories.

Schools of Thought

The recent narrative medicine movement owes much to Sacks's approach to neurology.* While Sacks appreciated his patients' subjective experiences and personal insights, he did not treat them merely as interesting stories; their narratives became part of his diagnoses and treatments. Although such an approach was unusual when the work appeared in 1985, neurology and medicine in general have since evolved towards encouraging doctors to listen to and interpret their patients' subjective stories.

As narrative medicine gained significant momentum and importance in the early 2000s, the approach became an emblem of such patient-doctor relationships. The physician Rita Charon,* a founder of the movement, cites Sacks as an early influence. But while Sacks sought to rethink how physicians and patients interacted, Charon took a broader approach—hoping to transform even more of the physician's relationships. In a 2000 article she wrote: "Adopting methods such as close reading of literature and reflective writing allows narrative medicine to examine and illuminate four of medicine's central narrative situations: physician and patient, physician and self, physician and colleagues, and physicians and society."[5]

Although Charon still stresses the need to reevaluate the ways in which physicians treat patients, she is optimistic that the field is moving in a more patient-centered direction. As she writes in her 2006 book *Narrative Medicine: Honoring the Stories of Illness*: "Medical schools, residency training programs, and professional societies have, in the past two or three decades, responded to the need to humanize medicine."[6]

In Current Scholarship

Proponents of narrative medicine frequently refer to Sacks's books—a clear indication that his work inspired them. However, the theoretical foundations behind the discipline were shaped by more academic works on the topic such as the psychiatrist* Arthur Kleinman's* 1988 book *The Illness Narratives*. Kleinman discussed many of the same themes as Sacks and made use of the narrative case study* style Sacks popularized. But Kleinman was also more explicit about why and how the medical community should change, writing: "When we place care at the center of medicine, we are forced to rethink medical training:

medical students and residents must be educated to perform the therapeutic tasks."[7] Nonetheless, *The Man Who Mistook His Wife* is acknowledged as an early promoter of this school of thought.

In the work, Sacks also criticizes his peers for defining neurological disorders as deficits and losses that impact well-being, and used his case studies as clever rebuttals. And eventually, the field came to respect Sacks's viewpoint; in 2013, a group of neuroscientists* wrote an article arguing that neurological disorders can indeed influence affected people in positive ways. Remarkably, they also acknowledged Sacks as one of the first thinkers who noticed this: "Losses are not always the only outcomes of nervous system insults. Such ideas are not new … noted Oliver Sacks."[8]

Sacks is also a leading popular science writer, and in part is responsible for the growing number of scientists and physicians writing about their work for a general readership. In a recent article on the rise of celebrity scientists, the health writer Julia Belluz noted: "Thanks to the work of Sacks and others—as well as to systemic shifts in science communication—doctors and medical researchers are often encouraged to communicate with a broader audience."[9]

NOTES

1 Oliver Sacks, *An Anthropologist on Mars: Seven Paradoxical Tales* (New York: Knopf, 1995), 11.

2 Sacks, *An Anthropologist*, 11.

3 Leonard Cassuto, "Oliver Sacks: The P.T. Barnum of the Postmodern World?" *American Quarterly*, 52, no. 2 (June 2000), 330.

4 G. Thomas Couser, *Vulnerable Subjects: Ethics and Life Writing* (New York: Cornell University Press, 2004), 78.

5 Rita Charon, "Narrative Medicine: A Model for Empathy, Reflection, Profession, and Trust," *Journal of the American Medical Association* 286, no. 15 (2001): 1897.

6 Rita Charon, *Narrative Medicine: Honoring the Stories of Illness* (New York: Oxford University Press, 2006), 7.

7   Arthur Kleinman, *The Illness Narratives: Suffering, Healing, and the Human Condition* (New York: Basic Books, 1988), 254.

8   Narinder Kapur et al., "Positive Clinical Neuroscience Explorations in Positive Neurology," *The Neuroscientist* 19, no. 4 (2013): 354–5.

9   Julia Belluz, "Why Oliver Sacks Was So Ambivalent About Becoming a Best-selling Author," *Vox*, July 17, 2015, accessed August 18, 2015, http://www.vox.com/2015/4/27/8503113/oliver-sacks-dr-oz.

MODULE 11
IMPACT AND INFLUENCE TODAY

KEY POINTS

- *The Man Who Mistook His Wife for a Hat* is an early and influential work promoting patient-centered* medical care and narrative case studies*—two approaches much more widely accepted today than in the 1980s.

- The text—along with a growing number of others with similar ideas—continues to challenge the medical community to adopt more patient-centered approaches.

- Medical researchers and physicians* planning approaches to patient care now typically incorporate patient-centered and narrative methods.

Position

Although Oliver Sacks's *The Man Who Mistook His Wife for a Hat* is not significantly debated today, Sacks continued until the end of his life to promote many of the themes found in the text. And so it represents an early work in a genre that promoted the use of narrative case studies, calling for physicians to honor their patients' biographical histories and experiences. The narrative medicine* movement supported by the physician Rita Charon* and the psychiatrist Arthur Kleinman* proposes changes in how physicians are educated, with doctors trained to listen to patients and apply the information they gather through personal interaction.

Pablo González Blasco,* a medical education specialist, recommends several of Sacks's works, including *The Man who Mistook His Wife*, as part of the curricula for educating and preparing medical doctors. In making the recommendation in a 2001 article, Blasco

> **❝** Nearly 30 years after *The Man Who Mistook His Wife for a Hat*, we live in its Gnostic universe, in thrall to brain science—its strangeness and its poetry as much as its clinical insights. **❞**
>
> David Wallace-Wells, *A Brain With a Heart*

wrote: "Since medicine is a profession dealing with people, any means to improve the understanding of the human being across all dimensions will be valuable in creating better doctors."[1]

The Man Who Mistook His Wife also retains relevance as a seminal work of popular science,* and remains one of the more respected such works. According to the communication scholar Declan Fahy,* known for his studies of science journalism, scientists engaging in public communication in the 1970s were dismissed as "second-class scientists, doing a lower form of work."[2] Many scientists believed it impossible to conduct first-class research and popularize their work at the same time. But Fahy thinks that stigma has faded, and Sacks is often acknowledged as the one responsible thanks to his production of quality works of popular science.

Interaction

The text, along with Sacks's later books, continues to challenge the medical community and experts in neurology in particular. Since its release, the influence and support of narrative medicine have grown, but in a seeming paradox, so has the positioning of evidence-based medicine*—the medical approach that dominated when Sacks wrote the text in the 1980s.

Sacks expressed ambivalence toward the evidence-based approach; technological advances in neuroimaging (visual representations of brain function) had always excited him. He recalled in his 2015 memoir *On the Move* that even early in his career, "new powers of imaging the brain ... [were] ... an exhilarating thought."[3] Yet he worried that the field had grown mechanical and inhumane—too reliant on journal findings, too dismissive of patients' insights.

Generally, however, Sacks did not challenge the findings of medical research or the value of the evidence-based approach. Neither do the leaders of the narrative medicine approach, who often use evidence from empirical studies to support the efficacy of their approach. Rita Charon reported on such studies in a 2000 article, writing: "Adding to early evidence of the usefulness of narrative practices, rigorous ethnographic and outcomes studies using samples of adequate size and control have been undertaken to ascertain the influences on students, physicians, and patients of narrative practices."[4]

Physicians supporting Sacks's approach or narrative medicine generally also rely on evidence to inform their decision-making. They do not wish to remove the science from medicine, but to revive a personal approach. Charon wrote that "A scientifically competent medicine alone cannot help a patient grapple with the loss of health or find meaning in suffering."[5] Valuing both approaches, Charon wrote, "Along with scientific ability, physicians need the ability to listen to the narratives of the patient, grasp and honor their meanings, and be moved to act on the patient's behalf."[6]

The Continuing Debate

Since the 1980s, the medical community has adopted a more patient-centered approach, arrived at through the growing acceptance of narrative medicine, and the addition of medical school curricula on physician-patient relationships.

While some in the profession continue to resist such changes, many accept these newer methods as needed—and not necessarily coming at the expense of the more ingrained, evidence-based approach. "Facts and figures are essential, but insufficient, to translate the data and promote the acceptance of evidence-based practices and policies," wrote the physicians and authors Zachary F. Meisel* and Jason Karlawish* in a 2011 commentary.[7]

They also reported that "evidence from social psychology research suggests that narratives, when compared with reporting statistical evidence alone, can have uniquely persuasive effects in overcoming preconceived beliefs and cognitive biases."[8] Their prevailing argument was that narrative and evidence-based medicine do not compete but complement one another; and the evidence supports such a claim.

Even one of the lead figures promoting evidence-based medicine, David L. Sackett,* wrote in a widely cited 1996 manifesto that this approach should especially entail an "increased expertise … in more effective and efficient diagnosis and in the more thoughtful identification and compassionate use of individual patients' predicaments, rights, and preferences in making clinical decisions about their care."[9]

Although the push for an inclusion of narrative medicine in the field was much bigger than *The Man Who Mistook His Wife,* there is no doubt that Sacks served as an important early contributor to what became a more respected aspect of medical practice.

NOTES

1   Pablo González Blasco, "Literature and Movies for Medical Students," *Family Medicine–Kansas City* 33, no. 6 (2001): 426.

2   Julia Belluz, "Why Oliver Sacks Was So Ambivalent About Becoming a Best-selling Author," *Vox,* July 17, 2015, accessed August 18, 2015, http://www.vox.com/2015/4/27/8503113/oliver-sacks-dr-oz.

3   Oliver Sacks, *On the Move: A Life* (New York: Alfred A. Knopf, 2015), 338.

4   Rita Charon, "Narrative Medicine: A Model for Empathy, Reflection, Profession, and Trust," *Journal of the American Medical Association* 286, no. 15 (2001): 1897.

5   Charon, *Narrative Medicine*, 1899.

6   Charon, *Narrative Medicice*, 1899.

7   Zachary F. Meisel and Jason Karlawish. "Narrative vs. Evidence-based
     Medicine—And, Not Or." *Journal of the American Medical Association* 306,
     no. 18 (2011): 2022.

8   Meisel and Karlawish, "Narrative vs. Evidence-based Medicine," 2022.

9   David L. Sackett et al., "Evidence Based Medicine: What It Is and What It
     Isn't," *British Medical Journal* 312, no. 7023 (1996): 71.

MODULE 12
WHERE NEXT?

KEY POINTS

- *The Man Who Mistook His Wife for a Hat* will serve as a valuable read for both the public and the medical community; and may find renewed value as neuroscientists* unlock new findings about the brain and mind.

- A seminal work for the narrative medicine* movement, the work may experience a new wave of influence as neuroscientists begin studying many of the topics Sacks discussed.

- The text was in ways ahead of its time, foreshadowing popular movements in medicine, neuroscience, and popular science* writing.

Potential

Oliver Sacks's *The Man Who Mistook His Wife for a Hat* has the potential to introduce neurological disorders to both lay readers and students new to the field. More than 30 years after its publication, it is still widely read by the general public, present in the popular media, and frequently used in educational settings—even to the point where it is recommended reading for medical students. And given the similarities between the themes in *The Man Who Mistook His Wife* and narrative medicine, the book may be seen as a quintessential volume in any reader's narrative medicine library.

Furthermore, neuroscience (the scientific study of the brain and nervous system), which greatly informs neurology* (the medical treatment of the kinds of conditions that Sacks describes), has learned an enormous amount since the publication of *The Man Who Mistook*

> **❝** Guideline developers and regulatory scientists must recognize, adapt, and deploy narrative to explain the science of guidelines to patients and families, health care professionals, and policy makers to promote their optimal understanding, uptake, and use. **❞**
>
> Zachary F. Meisel and Jason Karlawish, "Narrative vs. Evidence-Based Medicine—And, Not Or"

His Wife. In fact, recent findings in neuroscience support some of the more abstract ideas in the work, and Sacks's later publications.

Part of Sacks's idea of the "neurology of identity,"[1] for example, was that aspects of the mind, such as memory, should be described less as discrete units of memory and more like "scripts and scores"[2] that integrate one's identity, past, and imagination. The science writer Steve Silberman* noted the prescience of such a view: "In his books, Sacks has long anticipated this revisioning of the mind from a passive, ghostly decoder of stimuli to an interactive, adaptive, and endlessly innovative participant in the creation of our world."[3]

It was once believed that neurons* were the concrete units that held individual memories. But more recently, neuroscientific research has found that memories require the convergence of multiple brain areas, a process Silberman described as "like a richly interconnected network of stories, rather than an archive of static files"[4]—and more analogous to Sacks's view.

Future Directions
Promoters of narrative medicine such as Rita Charon* will shape the work's future influence in training physicians, as will prominent figures who promote changes to medical training curricula and general approaches to physician–patient relationships such as David M. Eddy.* But *The Man Who Mistook His Wife,* along with Sacks's broader

collection of work, already plays a crucial role in the movement and this is likely to continue.

Neuroscientists may revisit the work, along with Sacks's idea of the neurology of identity and the role narrative plays in researching the mind and consciousness.* In their popular introductory text to neuroscience, Mark Solms* and Oliver Turnbull* discuss changing approaches to the field: "The 'subjective' approach to mental science (psychoanalysis)* split off from the 'objective' approach (the neurosciences)."[5] The primary reason for this split, they contend, was that "it was not possible to learn anything useful about the mind—the *real* mind, in Oliver Sacks's sense—using the neuroscientific methods that were available at that time."[6]

But as Solms, Turnbull and many others now attest, neuroscientific methods, technologies, and ideas now allow doctors and researchers to study a person's subjective experience. Sacks was optimistic that Solms and Turnbull, or some future pioneer, would infuse modern neuroscience with the combined neurology and psychology that he and his mentor Alexander R. Luria* championed. Stating as much, Sacks wrote in the forward to Solms and Turnbull's text: "Solms's approach … [is] to make the most detailed neuropsychological* examination of patients with brain damage and then to submit them to a model psychoanalysis … to bring the mechanisms of the brain and the inner world of the patient together."[7]

Summary

The Man Who Mistook His Wife for a Hat is an important book and a seminal work of neurology and popular science for two reasons.

First, at a time when rare neurological disorders were confined to the specialist field of neurology, Sacks depicted them in a captivating way, while introducing them to the general public. He did so by portraying the patients as literary heroes and heroines, turning their struggles into tales that used poetic language a lay reader could easily grasp.

Second, Sacks challenged neurological conventions by relying on multiple perspectives, from his knowledge as a medical specialist to personal insights influenced by fields such as philosophy, literature, psychology, and art. This made the book relevant in the context of multiple disciplines.

The book's overall influence is both practical and theoretical. On the practical side, the text has been important in educating medical students; it serves as introductory reading used to make them familiar with rare neurological disorders and with how pathological brain functioning can impair human thinking and behavior. Similarly, the book appears on the reading lists for students of psychology at universities across the world. It remains a classic exploration of the relationship between the human brain and psychological qualities such as the mind, emotions, or identity; as a result, it is especially useful for undergraduate psychology students who hope to learn how the brain shapes human psychological functioning.

In the theoretical realm, where the book has exerted less influence, it is still regarded as an excellent example of the increasingly popular approach of narrative medicine. And in the decades to come, *The Man Who Mistook His Wife* and Sacks's broader body of work may find renewed appeal among neuroscientists just beginning to explore the more abstract concepts Sacks favored—the self, identity, and consciousness.

In making the case for patient-centered, narrative medicine, Sacks delivered a striking work of science and art that not only depicted neurology patients in a new light but also changed the course of neurology itself.

NOTES

1   Oliver Sacks, *The Man Who Mistook His Wife for a Hat and Other Clinical Tales* (New York: Touchstone, 1998), VIII.

2   Sacks, *The Man Who Mistook His Wife*, 139.

3   Steve Silberman, "The Fully Immersive Mind of Oliver Sacks," *Wired*, October 2004, accessed August 18, 2015, http://archive.wired.com/wired/archive/10.04/sacks_pr.html.

4   Silberman, "The Fully Immersive Mind of Oliver Sacks."

5   Mark Solms and Oliver Turnbull, *The Brain and the Inner World: An Introduction to the Neuroscience of Subjective Experience* (London: Karnac Books, 2002), 5.

6   Solms and Turnbull, *Neuroscience*, 5.

7   Solms and Turnbull, *Neuroscience*, ix.

GLOSSARY

GLOSSARY OF TERMS

Agnosia: the inability to interpret sensations, and hence to recognize things; it typically results from brain damage.

Amphetamine: a drug that stimulates the central nervous system.

Case study: a detailed description of the course of a disorder in a single patient.

Classical neurology: what Sacks referred to as the traditional approach to neurology throughout the twentieth century.

Clinical expertise: the clinician's accumulated experience, education, and clinical skills.

Clinical study: empirical research study that tests the effectiveness and safety of medical treatments on humans.

Consciousness: being aware of an external object or something in oneself.

Encephalitis lethargica: a neurological condition (also known as "sleepy sickness") caused by a virus and characterized by headache and drowsiness, leading to coma. Sacks wrote about his experiences with patients suffering from this disorder in his 1973 book *Awakenings*.

Etiology: the origin and causes of a medical condition.

Evidence-based medicine: an approach to medical practice that largely relies on empirical research findings, often from clinical studies, to inform decisions about diagnoses and treatments.

Existential: concerned with existence, especially human existence.

Hallucinations: the sensory perception of something that is not truly present. Most often hallucinations are visual or auditory.

Holistic: associated with the understanding that all parts of any issue are connected and can only be understood by looking at the whole. In medicine a holistic treatment takes into account social and mental elements and is not limited to dealing with bodily symptoms.

Intracranial lesion: damaged brain tissue due to injury or disease.

L-dopa: a chemical that effectively treats neurological movement disorders, such as Parkinson's disease.

Left hemisphere of the brain: the left half of the human brain. Some neurological disorders involving speech are more likely associated with damage to this half.

Localization of functions: a phrase referring to different areas in the brain being specialized for different functions.

LSD: an acronym for lysergic acid diethylamide, a chemical often used for its hallucinogenic and psychedelic effects.

Mania: a mental/psychological condition involving periods of excitability and hyperactivity, as well as delusions and euphoria.

Morning glory seeds: a plant seed sometimes ingested for its hallucinogenic and psychedelic effects.

Motor control: the process by which the neuromuscular system activates and coordinates muscles and limbs.

Motor impulse: electrical signals between nerve cells involved in motor control.

Narrative medicine: a medical approach that recognizes the value of people's narratives in clinical practice, research, and education. Oliver Sacks popularized this technique in *The Man Who Mistook His Wife for a Hat*.

Nervous system: the part of a human body composed of specialized cells known as neurons that guides the functioning of the body and mind. It contains organs such as the brain.

Neurology: the branch of medicine that deals with diseases and disorders of the nervous system.

Neurological condition/disorder: any disturbance of the normal functioning of the nervous system that hampers people in coping with everyday life by altering thinking, memory, sensation, or other abilities.

Neurons: specialized cells transmitting nerve impulses and involved in many brain functions.

Neuropsychology: a branch of psychology that often focuses on how brain injuries or illnesses affect cognitive functions and behaviors.

Neuroscience/neuroscientist: the biological study of the nervous system.

Parkinson's disease: a condition involving the degeneration of the central nervous system that results in loss of motor control.

Patient-centered: an approach to medical care in which physicians include the patient's desires, preferences, values, and circumstances when making decisions about treatment.

Physician: a qualified medical practitioner.

Popular science: an interpretation of science aimed at a general audience.

Propositional calculus: a branch of mathematical logic.

Prosopagnosia: a neurological condition that results in the loss of ability to recognize and understand certain objects, particularly human faces. Sacks suffered from this condition.

Psychiatry: a branch of medicine focusing on mental illness.

Psychoanalysis: a form of talk therapy developed by Sigmund Freud. It is popularly used to treat mental illness through examination of the conscious and unconscious aspects of a patient's mind.

Reminiscence: the enjoyable recollection of past events.

Right hemisphere of the brain: the right half of the human brain. Some neurological disorders involving vision are more likely associated with damage to this half.

Schizophrenia: a brain disorder in which people interpret reality abnormally.

Seizure: an abnormal and sudden surge of electrical activity in the brain. It affects the sufferer's ability to control certain behaviors, and can result in unconsciousness.

Temporal lobe: one of the four major lobes of the brain and involved with functions associated with sound.

Tourette's syndrome: a neurological condition that results in involuntary and typically undesired movements and vocalizations.

PEOPLE MENTIONED IN THE TEXT

Pablo González Blasco (b. 1957) is a Spanish-born professor of family medicine in Brazil. He is known for his research and teaching on medical ethics in the context of family medicine and medical education.

Leonard Cassuto (b. 1960) is an American author and professor of American literature at Fordham University. He is known for his writings about disability.

Rita Charon (b. 1949) is an American physician and director of the program in narrative medicine at Columbia University. She is known as the founder of the narrative medicine approach.

Alexander Cockburn (1941–2012) was an Irish American political journalist and writer. He is known for his political writings and commentary.

G. Thomas Couser was an American professor of English at Hofstra University who retired in 2011. He is known for his writings on disability studies.

Antonio Damasio (b. 1944) is a Portuguese professor of neuroscience at the University of Southern California. He is known for his work on the relationship between the brain and consciousness.

Hanna Damasio (b. 1942) is a Portuguese professor of neuroscience at the University of Southern California. She is known for her work using neuroimaging to examine the structure and function of the brain.

David M. Eddy (b. 1941) is an American physician and healthcare analyst. He is known for his work on medical guidelines and evidence-based medicine.

Declan Fahy is an Irish professor of communication at American University. He is known for his work examining science journalism.

Sigmund Freud (1856–1939) was an Austrian neurologist and psychologist and founder of psychoanalysis.

Hildegard of Bingen (1098–1179), also known as Saint Hildegard, was a German intellectual. A Benedictine abbess, she is known for her religious writings and was canonized by the Roman Catholic Church.

John Hughlings Jackson (1835–1911) was an English neurologist. He is known for establishing neurology as a science.

Jason Karlawish is an American physician and professor of medicine at the University of Pennsylvania. He is known for his work on medical bioethics and health policy.

Arthur Kleinman (b. 1941) is an American psychiatrist and is currently the Esther and Sidney Rabb Professor of Anthropology at Harvard University. He is known for his work on international public health.

Edward Liveing (1832–1919) was an English physician. He is known for his work on the study of migraines.

Alexander R. Luria (1902–77) was a Soviet neuropsychologist. He is known for his case studies on subjects with extreme neurological conditions.

Zachary F. Meisel is an American physician and scholar at the University of Pennsylvania. He is known for writing about medical issues in the popular press.

Geoff Norman is a Canadian professor of clinical epidemiology and biostatistics at McMaster University. He is known for his work on physician reasoning and decision-making.

William H. Oldendorf (1925–92) was an American neurologist. He is known for developing neuroimaging techniques.

Wilder Penfield (1891–1976) was a Canadian neurosurgeon. He is known for uncovering the function of several regions of the brain.

Pablo Picasso (1881–1973) was a Spanish artist. He is known as one of the greatest painters and artists of the twentieth century.

David L. Sackett (1934–2015) was a Canadian physician. He was known for his work examining the evidence-based approach to medicine.

Sandra Schor (1932–90) was an American writer. She is known for her scholarly work on composition.

Tom Shakespeare (b. 1966) is a senior lecturer at the University of East Anglia's Norwich Medical School. A disability-rights activist, his primary research interests are in disability studies, medical sociology, and social and ethical aspects of genetics.

Steve Silberman is an American writer. He is known for his writings on popular science and autism.

Mark Solms (b. 1961) is a South African psychoanalyst and professor at the University of Cape Town. He is known for his work on neuropsychoanalysis.

Oliver Turnbull is a South African neuropsychologist and professor at Bangor University in the United Kingdom. He is known for his work on agnosia.

Alan G. Wasserstein is an American physician and professor of medicine at the University of Pennsylvania. He is known for his work on the history of medicine.

WORKS CITED

WORKS CITED

Belluz, Julia. "Why Oliver Sacks Was So Ambivalent About Becoming a Bestselling Author." *Vox*, July 17, 2015. Accessed August 18, 2015. http://www.vox.com/2015/4/27/8503113/oliver-sacks-dr-oz.

Blasco, Pablo González. "Literature and Movies for Medical Students." *Family Medicine-Kansas City* 33, no. 6 (2001): 426–8.

Brawarsky, Sandee. "Street Neurologist With a Sense of Wonder." *The Lancet* 350, no. 9084 (1997): 1092–3.

Burrell, Lisa. "Life's Work: Oliver Sacks." *Harvard Business Review*, November 2010. Accessed August 18, 2015. https://hbr.org/2010/11/lifes-work-oliver-sacks.

Cassuto, Leonard. "Oliver Sacks: The P.T. Barnum of the Postmodern World?" *American Quarterly* 52, no. 2 (June 2000), 326–33.

Charon, Rita. "Narrative Medicine: A Model for Empathy, Reflection, Profession, and Trust." *Journal of the American Medical Association* 286, no. 15 (2001): 1897–1902.

Narrative Medicine: Honoring the Stories of Illness. New York: Oxford University Press, 2006.

Cockburn, Alexander. "Wonders in Barmy Land." *Nation* 256 (June 14, 1993): 822–3.

Couser, Thomas G. *Vulnerable Subjects: Ethics and Life Writing*. New York: Cornell University Press, 2004.

Cowles, Gregory. "Oliver Sacks, Neurologist Who Wrote About the Brain's Quirks, Dies at 82." *New York Times*, August 15, 2015. Accessed September 22, 2015. http://www.nytimes.com/2015/08/31/science/oliver-sacks-dies-at-82-neurologist-and-author-explored-the-brains-quirks.html.

Eddy, David M. "Variations in Physician Practice: The Role of Uncertainty." *Health Affairs* 3, no. 2 (1984): 74–89.

Flynn, Dale, Susan Palo, and Oliver Sacks. "An Interview with Oliver Sacks." *Writing on the Edge* 1, no. 1 (Fall, 1989): 99–106.

Freud, Sigmund. *Recommendations to Physicians Practising Psycho-Analysis*. London: The Hogarth Press, 1912.

Hoffmann, Roald. "The Metaphor, Unchained: Scientists Improve Their Craft by Writing About it." *American Scientist*, September-October 2006. Accessed September 24, 2015. http://www.americanscientist.org/issues/pub/the-metaphor-unchained.

Kahy, Declan. *The New Celebrity Scientists: Out of the Lab and into the Limelight*. London: Rowman & Littlefield, 2015.

Kapur, Narinder, Jonathan Cole, Tom Manly, Indre Viskontas, Aafke Ninteman, Lynn Hasher, and Alvaro Pascual-Leone. "Positive Clinical Neuroscience: Explorations in Positive Neurology." *The Neuroscientist* 19, no. 4 (2013): 354–69.

Kleinman, Arthur. *The Illness Narratives: Suffering, Healing, and the Human Condition*. New York: Basic Books, 1988.

Luria, Alexander R. *The Man With a Shattered World: The History of a Brain Wound*. Cambridge: Harvard University Press, 1972.

The Mind of a Mnemonist: A Little Book About a Vast Memory. Translated by Lynn Solotaroff. New York: Basic Books, 1987.

Marshall, John C. "In the Region of Lost Minds." *New York Times*, March 2, 1986. Accessed September 22, 2015. https://www.nytimes.com/books/98/12/06/specials/sacks-mistook.html.

Meisel, Zachary F. and Jason Karlawish. "Narrative vs. Evidence-based Medicine—And, Not Or." *Journal of the American Medical Association* 306, no. 18 (2011): 2022–3.

Mergenthaler, Daniela. "Oliver Sacks—A Neurologist Explores the Lifeworld." *Medicine, Health Care and Philosophy* 3 (2000): 275–83.

Norman, Geoffrey. "Research in Clinical Reasoning: Past History and Current Trends." *Medical Education* 39, no. 4 (2005): 418–27.

Sackett, David L., William M. Rosenberg, J.A. Gray, R. Brian Haynes, and W. Scott Richardson. "Evidence Based Medicine: What It Is and What It Isn't." *British Medical Journal* 312, no. 7023 (1996): 71–2.

Sacks, Oliver. "Altered States: Self-experiments in Chemistry." *The New Yorker*, August 27, 2012. Accessed August 18, 2015. http://www.newyorker.com/magazine/2012/08/27/altered-states-3.

An Anthropologist on Mars: Seven Paradoxical Tales. New York: Knopf, 1995.

Awakenings. New York: Vintage Books, 1990.

Hallucinations. New York: Vintage Books, 2013.

Musicophilia: Tales of Music and the Brain. New York: Vintage Books, 2007.

On the Move: A Life. New York: Alfred A. Knopf, 2015.

The Man Who Mistook His Wife for a Hat and Other Clinical Tales. New York: Touchstone, 1998.

Schor, Sandra. "Writing across the Disciplines: Respecting the Untranslatable." Paper presented at the 38th Annual Meeting of the Conference on College Composition and Communication, Atlanta, GA, March 19–21, 1987.

Silberman, Steve. "The Fully Immersive Mind of Oliver Sacks." *Wired*, October, 2004. Accessed August 18, 2015. http://archive.wired.com/wired/archive/10.04/sacks_pr.html

Solms, Mark, and Oliver Turnbull. *The Brain and the Inner World: An Introduction to the Neuroscience of Subjective Experience*. London: Karnac Books, 2002.

Sutherland, Stuart. "Review of Sacks, *The Man Who Mistook His Wife for a Hat*." *Nature* 318, no. 609 (1985): 19.

The American Society of Neuroimaging. "History of Neuroimaging." Accessed August 18, 2015. http://www.asnweb.org/i4a/pages/index.cfm?pageid=3334.

Tyler, Kenneth, George K. York, David A. Steinberg, Michael S. Okun, Michelle Steinbach, Richard Satran, Edward J. Fine, Tara Manteghi, Thomas P. Bleck, Jerry W. Swanson, Shrikant Mishra, Kimford J. Meador, David B. Clifford, James F. Toole, and Lella Melson. "Part 2: History of 20th-Century Neurology: Decade by Decade." *Annals of Neurology* 53, no. S4 (2003): S27–S45.

Wallace-Wells, David. "A Brain With a Heart." *New York Magazine*, November 4, 2012. Accessed September 22, 2015. http://nymag.com/news/features/oliver-sacks-2012-11/.

Wasserstein, Alan G. "Toward a Romantic Science: The Work of Oliver Sacks." *Annals of Internal Medicine* 109, no. 5 (1988): 440–4.

THE MACAT LIBRARY
BY DISCIPLINE

AFRICANA STUDIES

Chinua Achebe's *An Image of Africa: Racism in Conrad's Heart of Darkness*
W. E. B. Du Bois's *The Souls of Black Folk*
Zora Neale Huston's *Characteristics of Negro Expression*
Martin Luther King Jr's *Why We Can't Wait*
Toni Morrison's *Playing in the Dark: Whiteness in the American Literary Imagination*

ANTHROPOLOGY

Arjun Appadurai's *Modernity at Large: Cultural Dimensions of Globalisation*
Philippe Ariès's *Centuries of Childhood*
Franz Boas's *Race, Language and Culture*
Kim Chan & Renée Mauborgne's *Blue Ocean Strategy*
Jared Diamond's *Guns, Germs & Steel: the Fate of Human Societies*
Jared Diamond's *Collapse: How Societies Choose to Fail or Survive*
E. E. Evans-Pritchard's *Witchcraft, Oracles and Magic Among the Azande*
James Ferguson's *The Anti-Politics Machine*
Clifford Geertz's *The Interpretation of Cultures*
David Graeber's *Debt: the First 5000 Years*
Karen Ho's *Liquidated: An Ethnography of Wall Street*
Geert Hofstede's *Culture's Consequences: Comparing Values, Behaviors, Institutes and Organizations across Nations*
Claude Lévi-Strauss's *Structural Anthropology*
Jay Macleod's *Ain't No Makin' It: Aspirations and Attainment in a Low-Income Neighborhood*
Saba Mahmood's *The Politics of Piety: The Islamic Revival and the Feminist Subject*
Marcel Mauss's *The Gift*

BUSINESS

Jean Lave & Etienne Wenger's *Situated Learning*
Theodore Levitt's *Marketing Myopia*
Burton G. Malkiel's *A Random Walk Down Wall Street*
Douglas McGregor's *The Human Side of Enterprise*
Michael Porter's *Competitive Strategy: Creating and Sustaining Superior Performance*
John Kotter's *Leading Change*
C. K. Prahalad & Gary Hamel's *The Core Competence of the Corporation*

CRIMINOLOGY

Michelle Alexander's *The New Jim Crow: Mass Incarceration in the Age of Colorblindness*
Michael R. Gottfredson & Travis Hirschi's *A General Theory of Crime*
Richard Herrnstein & Charles A. Murray's *The Bell Curve: Intelligence and Class Structure in American Life*
Elizabeth Loftus's *Eyewitness Testimony*
Jay Macleod's *Ain't No Makin' It: Aspirations and Attainment in a Low-Income Neighborhood*
Philip Zimbardo's *The Lucifer Effect*

ECONOMICS

Janet Abu-Lughod's *Before European Hegemony*
Ha-Joon Chang's *Kicking Away the Ladder*
David Brion Davis's *The Problem of Slavery in the Age of Revolution*
Milton Friedman's *The Role of Monetary Policy*
Milton Friedman's *Capitalism and Freedom*
David Graeber's *Debt: the First 5000 Years*
Friedrich Hayek's *The Road to Serfdom*
Karen Ho's *Liquidated: An Ethnography of Wall Street*

John Maynard Keynes's *The General Theory of Employment, Interest and Money*
Charles P. Kindleberger's *Manias, Panics and Crashes*
Robert Lucas's *Why Doesn't Capital Flow from Rich to Poor Countries?*
Burton G. Malkiel's *A Random Walk Down Wall Street*
Thomas Robert Malthus's *An Essay on the Principle of Population*
Karl Marx's *Capital*
Thomas Piketty's *Capital in the Twenty-First Century*
Amartya Sen's *Development as Freedom*
Adam Smith's *The Wealth of Nations*
Nassim Nicholas Taleb's *The Black Swan: The Impact of the Highly Improbable*
Amos Tversky's & Daniel Kahneman's *Judgment under Uncertainty: Heuristics and Biases*
Mahbub Ul Haq's *Reflections on Human Development*
Max Weber's *The Protestant Ethic and the Spirit of Capitalism*

FEMINISM AND GENDER STUDIES

Judith Butler's *Gender Trouble*
Simone De Beauvoir's *The Second Sex*
Michel Foucault's *History of Sexuality*
Betty Friedan's *The Feminine Mystique*
Saba Mahmood's *The Politics of Piety: The Islamic Revival and the Feminist Subject*
Joan Wallach Scott's *Gender and the Politics of History*
Mary Wollstonecraft's *A Vindication of the Rights of Women*
Virginia Woolf's *A Room of One's Own*

GEOGRAPHY

The Brundtland Report's *Our Common Future*
Rachel Carson's *Silent Spring*
Charles Darwin's *On the Origin of Species*
James Ferguson's *The Anti-Politics Machine*
Jane Jacobs's *The Death and Life of Great American Cities*
James Lovelock's *Gaia: A New Look at Life on Earth*
Amartya Sen's *Development as Freedom*
Mathis Wackernagel & William Rees's *Our Ecological Footprint*

HISTORY

Janet Abu-Lughod's *Before European Hegemony*
Benedict Anderson's *Imagined Communities*
Bernard Bailyn's *The Ideological Origins of the American Revolution*
Hanna Batatu's *The Old Social Classes And The Revolutionary Movements Of Iraq*
Christopher Browning's *Ordinary Men: Reserve Police Batallion 101 and the Final Solution in Poland*
Edmund Burke's *Reflections on the Revolution in France*
William Cronon's *Nature's Metropolis: Chicago And The Great West*
Alfred W. Crosby's *The Columbian Exchange*
Hamid Dabashi's *Iran: A People Interrupted*
David Brion Davis's *The Problem of Slavery in the Age of Revolution*
Nathalie Zemon Davis's *The Return of Martin Guerre*
Jared Diamond's *Guns, Germs & Steel: the Fate of Human Societies*
Frank Dikotter's *Mao's Great Famine*
John W Dower's *War Without Mercy: Race And Power In The Pacific War*
W. E. B. Du Bois's *The Souls of Black Folk*
Richard J. Evans's *In Defence of History*
Lucien Febvre's *The Problem of Unbelief in the 16th Century*
Sheila Fitzpatrick's *Everyday Stalinism*

Eric Foner's *Reconstruction: America's Unfinished Revolution, 1863-1877*
Michel Foucault's *Discipline and Punish*
Michel Foucault's *History of Sexuality*
Francis Fukuyama's *The End of History and the Last Man*
John Lewis Gaddis's *We Now Know: Rethinking Cold War History*
Ernest Gellner's *Nations and Nationalism*
Eugene Genovese's *Roll, Jordan, Roll: The World the Slaves Made*
Carlo Ginzburg's *The Night Battles*
Daniel Goldhagen's *Hitler's Willing Executioners*
Jack Goldstone's *Revolution and Rebellion in the Early Modern World*
Antonio Gramsci's *The Prison Notebooks*
Alexander Hamilton, John Jay & James Madison's *The Federalist Papers*
Christopher Hill's *The World Turned Upside Down*
Carole Hillenbrand's *The Crusades: Islamic Perspectives*
Thomas Hobbes's *Leviathan*
Eric Hobsbawm's *The Age Of Revolution*
John A. Hobson's *Imperialism: A Study*
Albert Hourani's *History of the Arab Peoples*
Samuel P. Huntington's *The Clash of Civilizations and the Remaking of World Order*
C. L. R. James's *The Black Jacobins*
Tony Judt's *Postwar: A History of Europe Since 1945*
Ernst Kantorowicz's *The King's Two Bodies: A Study in Medieval Political Theology*
Paul Kennedy's *The Rise and Fall of the Great Powers*
Ian Kershaw's *The "Hitler Myth": Image and Reality in the Third Reich*
John Maynard Keynes's *The General Theory of Employment, Interest and Money*
Charles P. Kindleberger's *Manias, Panics and Crashes*
Martin Luther King Jr's *Why We Can't Wait*
Henry Kissinger's *World Order: Reflections on the Character of Nations and the Course of History*
Thomas Kuhn's *The Structure of Scientific Revolutions*
Georges Lefebvre's *The Coming of the French Revolution*
John Locke's *Two Treatises of Government*
Niccolò Machiavelli's *The Prince*
Thomas Robert Malthus's *An Essay on the Principle of Population*
Mahmood Mamdani's *Citizen and Subject: Contemporary Africa And The Legacy Of Late Colonialism*
Karl Marx's *Capital*
Stanley Milgram's *Obedience to Authority*
John Stuart Mill's *On Liberty*
Thomas Paine's *Common Sense*
Thomas Paine's *Rights of Man*
Geoffrey Parker's *Global Crisis: War, Climate Change and Catastrophe in the Seventeenth Century*
Jonathan Riley-Smith's *The First Crusade and the Idea of Crusading*
Jean-Jacques Rousseau's *The Social Contract*
Joan Wallach Scott's *Gender and the Politics of History*
Theda Skocpol's *States and Social Revolutions*
Adam Smith's *The Wealth of Nations*
Timothy Snyder's *Bloodlands: Europe Between Hitler and Stalin*
Sun Tzu's *The Art of War*
Keith Thomas's *Religion and the Decline of Magic*
Thucydides's *The History of the Peloponnesian War*
Frederick Jackson Turner's *The Significance of the Frontier in American History*
Odd Arne Westad's *The Global Cold War: Third World Interventions And The Making Of Our Times*

LITERATURE

Chinua Achebe's *An Image of Africa: Racism in Conrad's Heart of Darkness*
Roland Barthes's *Mythologies*
Homi K. Bhabha's *The Location of Culture*
Judith Butler's *Gender Trouble*
Simone De Beauvoir's *The Second Sex*
Ferdinand De Saussure's *Course in General Linguistics*
T. S. Eliot's *The Sacred Wood: Essays on Poetry and Criticism*
Zora Neale Huston's *Characteristics of Negro Expression*
Toni Morrison's *Playing in the Dark: Whiteness in the American Literary Imagination*
Edward Said's *Orientalism*
Gayatri Chakravorty Spivak's *Can the Subaltern Speak?*
Mary Wollstonecraft's *A Vindication of the Rights of Women*
Virginia Woolf's *A Room of One's Own*

PHILOSOPHY

Elizabeth Anscombe's *Modern Moral Philosophy*
Hannah Arendt's *The Human Condition*
Aristotle's *Metaphysics*
Aristotle's *Nicomachean Ethics*
Edmund Gettier's *Is Justified True Belief Knowledge?*
Georg Wilhelm Friedrich Hegel's *Phenomenology of Spirit*
David Hume's *Dialogues Concerning Natural Religion*
David Hume's *The Enquiry for Human Understanding*
Immanuel Kant's *Religion within the Boundaries of Mere Reason*
Immanuel Kant's *Critique of Pure Reason*
Søren Kierkegaard's *The Sickness Unto Death*
Søren Kierkegaard's *Fear and Trembling*
C. S. Lewis's *The Abolition of Man*
Alasdair MacIntyre's *After Virtue*
Marcus Aurelius's *Meditations*
Friedrich Nietzsche's *On the Genealogy of Morality*
Friedrich Nietzsche's *Beyond Good and Evil*
Plato's *Republic*
Plato's *Symposium*
Jean-Jacques Rousseau's *The Social Contract*
Gilbert Ryle's *The Concept of Mind*
Baruch Spinoza's *Ethics*
Sun Tzu's *The Art of War*
Ludwig Wittgenstein's *Philosophical Investigations*

POLITICS

Benedict Anderson's *Imagined Communities*
Aristotle's *Politics*
Bernard Bailyn's *The Ideological Origins of the American Revolution*
Edmund Burke's *Reflections on the Revolution in France*
John C. Calhoun's *A Disquisition on Government*
Ha-Joon Chang's *Kicking Away the Ladder*
Hamid Dabashi's *Iran: A People Interrupted*
Hamid Dabashi's *Theology of Discontent: The Ideological Foundation of the Islamic Revolution in Iran*
Robert Dahl's *Democracy and its Critics*
Robert Dahl's *Who Governs?*
David Brion Davis's *The Problem of Slavery in the Age of Revolution*

Alexis De Tocqueville's *Democracy in America*
James Ferguson's *The Anti-Politics Machine*
Frank Dikotter's *Mao's Great Famine*
Sheila Fitzpatrick's *Everyday Stalinism*
Eric Foner's *Reconstruction: America's Unfinished Revolution, 1863-1877*
Milton Friedman's *Capitalism and Freedom*
Francis Fukuyama's *The End of History and the Last Man*
John Lewis Gaddis's *We Now Know: Rethinking Cold War History*
Ernest Gellner's *Nations and Nationalism*
David Graeber's *Debt: the First 5000 Years*
Antonio Gramsci's *The Prison Notebooks*
Alexander Hamilton, John Jay & James Madison's *The Federalist Papers*
Friedrich Hayek's *The Road to Serfdom*
Christopher Hill's *The World Turned Upside Down*
Thomas Hobbes's *Leviathan*
John A. Hobson's *Imperialism: A Study*
Samuel P. Huntington's *The Clash of Civilizations and the Remaking of World Order*
Tony Judt's *Postwar: A History of Europe Since 1945*
David C. Kang's *China Rising: Peace, Power and Order in East Asia*
Paul Kennedy's *The Rise and Fall of Great Powers*
Robert Keohane's *After Hegemony*
Martin Luther King Jr.'s *Why We Can't Wait*
Henry Kissinger's *World Order: Reflections on the Character of Nations and the Course of History*
John Locke's *Two Treatises of Government*
Niccolò Machiavelli's *The Prince*
Thomas Robert Malthus's *An Essay on the Principle of Population*
Mahmood Mamdani's *Citizen and Subject: Contemporary Africa And The Legacy Of Late Colonialism*
Karl Marx's *Capital*
John Stuart Mill's *On Liberty*
John Stuart Mill's *Utilitarianism*
Hans Morgenthau's *Politics Among Nations*
Thomas Paine's *Common Sense*
Thomas Paine's *Rights of Man*
Thomas Piketty's *Capital in the Twenty-First Century*
Robert D. Putman's *Bowling Alone*
John Rawls's *Theory of Justice*
Jean-Jacques Rousseau's *The Social Contract*
Theda Skocpol's *States and Social Revolutions*
Adam Smith's *The Wealth of Nations*
Sun Tzu's *The Art of War*
Henry David Thoreau's *Civil Disobedience*
Thucydides's *The History of the Peloponnesian War*
Kenneth Waltz's *Theory of International Politics*
Max Weber's *Politics as a Vocation*
Odd Arne Westad's *The Global Cold War: Third World Interventions And The Making Of Our Times*

POSTCOLONIAL STUDIES

Roland Barthes's *Mythologies*
Frantz Fanon's *Black Skin, White Masks*
Homi K. Bhabha's *The Location of Culture*
Gustavo Gutiérrez's *A Theology of Liberation*
Edward Said's *Orientalism*
Gayatri Chakravorty Spivak's *Can the Subaltern Speak?*

PSYCHOLOGY

Gordon Allport's *The Nature of Prejudice*
Alan Baddeley & Graham Hitch's *Aggression: A Social Learning Analysis*
Albert Bandura's *Aggression: A Social Learning Analysis*
Leon Festinger's *A Theory of Cognitive Dissonance*
Sigmund Freud's *The Interpretation of Dreams*
Betty Friedan's *The Feminine Mystique*
Michael R. Gottfredson & Travis Hirschi's *A General Theory of Crime*
Eric Hoffer's *The True Believer: Thoughts on the Nature of Mass Movements*
William James's *Principles of Psychology*
Elizabeth Loftus's *Eyewitness Testimony*
A. H. Maslow's *A Theory of Human Motivation*
Stanley Milgram's *Obedience to Authority*
Steven Pinker's *The Better Angels of Our Nature*
Oliver Sacks's *The Man Who Mistook His Wife For a Hat*
Richard Thaler & Cass Sunstein's *Nudge: Improving Decisions About Health, Wealth and Happiness*
Amos Tversky's *Judgment under Uncertainty: Heuristics and Biases*
Philip Zimbardo's *The Lucifer Effect*

SCIENCE

Rachel Carson's *Silent Spring*
William Cronon's *Nature's Metropolis: Chicago And The Great West*
Alfred W. Crosby's *The Columbian Exchange*
Charles Darwin's *On the Origin of Species*
Richard Dawkin's *The Selfish Gene*
Thomas Kuhn's *The Structure of Scientific Revolutions*
Geoffrey Parker's *Global Crisis: War, Climate Change and Catastrophe in the Seventeenth Century*
Mathis Wackernagel & William Rees's *Our Ecological Footprint*

SOCIOLOGY

Michelle Alexander's *The New Jim Crow: Mass Incarceration in the Age of Colorblindness*
Gordon Allport's *The Nature of Prejudice*
Albert Bandura's *Aggression: A Social Learning Analysis*
Hanna Batatu's *The Old Social Classes And The Revolutionary Movements Of Iraq*
Ha-Joon Chang's *Kicking Away the Ladder*
W. E. B. Du Bois's *The Souls of Black Folk*
Émile Durkheim's *On Suicide*
Frantz Fanon's *Black Skin, White Masks*
Frantz Fanon's *The Wretched of the Earth*
Eric Foner's *Reconstruction: America's Unfinished Revolution, 1863-1877*
Eugene Genovese's *Roll, Jordan, Roll: The World the Slaves Made*
Jack Goldstone's *Revolution and Rebellion in the Early Modern World*
Antonio Gramsci's *The Prison Notebooks*
Richard Herrnstein & Charles A Murray's *The Bell Curve: Intelligence and Class Structure in American Life*
Eric Hoffer's *The True Believer: Thoughts on the Nature of Mass Movements*
Jane Jacobs's *The Death and Life of Great American Cities*
Robert Lucas's *Why Doesn't Capital Flow from Rich to Poor Countries?*
Jay Macleod's *Ain't No Makin' It: Aspirations and Attainment in a Low Income Neighborhood*
Elaine May's *Homeward Bound: American Families in the Cold War Era*
Douglas McGregor's *The Human Side of Enterprise*
C. Wright Mills's *The Sociological Imagination*

The Macat Library By Discipline

Thomas Piketty's *Capital in the Twenty-First Century*
Robert D. Putman's *Bowling Alone*
David Riesman's *The Lonely Crowd: A Study of the Changing American Character*
Edward Said's *Orientalism*
Joan Wallach Scott's *Gender and the Politics of History*
Theda Skocpol's *States and Social Revolutions*
Max Weber's *The Protestant Ethic and the Spirit of Capitalism*

THEOLOGY

Augustine's *Confessions*
Benedict's *Rule of St Benedict*
Gustavo Gutiérrez's *A Theology of Liberation*
Carole Hillenbrand's *The Crusades: Islamic Perspectives*
David Hume's *Dialogues Concerning Natural Religion*
Immanuel Kant's *Religion within the Boundaries of Mere Reason*
Ernst Kantorowicz's *The King's Two Bodies: A Study in Medieval Political Theology*
Søren Kierkegaard's *The Sickness Unto Death*
C. S. Lewis's *The Abolition of Man*
Saba Mahmood's *The Politics of Piety: The Islamic Revival and the Feminist Subject*
Baruch Spinoza's *Ethics*
Keith Thomas's *Religion and the Decline of Magic*

COMING SOON

Chris Argyris's *The Individual and the Organisation*
Seyla Benhabib's *The Rights of Others*
Walter Benjamin's *The Work Of Art in the Age of Mechanical Reproduction*
John Berger's *Ways of Seeing*
Pierre Bourdieu's *Outline of a Theory of Practice*
Mary Douglas's *Purity and Danger*
Roland Dworkin's *Taking Rights Seriously*
James G. March's *Exploration and Exploitation in Organisational Learning*
Ikujiro Nonaka's *A Dynamic Theory of Organizational Knowledge Creation*
Griselda Pollock's *Vision and Difference*
Amartya Sen's *Inequality Re-Examined*
Susan Sontag's *On Photography*
Yasser Tabbaa's *The Transformation of Islamic Art*
Ludwig von Mises's *Theory of Money and Credit*